Shakespeare and *Game of Thrones*

It is widely acknowledged that the hit franchise *Game of Thrones* is based on the Wars of the Roses, a bloody fifteenth-century civil war between feuding English families. In this book, Jeffrey R. Wilson shows how that connection was mediated by Shakespeare, and how a knowledge of the Shakespearean context enriches our understanding of the literary elements of *Game of Thrones*.

On the one hand, Shakespeare influenced *Game of Thrones* indirectly because his history plays significantly shaped the way the Wars of the Roses are now remembered, including the modern histories and historical fictions George R.R. Martin drew upon. On the other, *Game of Thrones* also responds to Shakespeare's first tetralogy directly by adapting several of its literary strategies (such as shifting perspectives, mixed genres, and metatheater) and tropes (including the stigmatized protagonist and the prince who was promised). Presenting new interviews with the *Game of Thrones* cast, and comparing contextual circumstances of composition—such as collaborative authorship and political currents—this book also lodges a series of provocations about writing and acting for the stage in the Elizabethan age and for the screen in the twenty-first century.

An essential read for fans of the franchise, as well as students and academics looking at Shakespeare and Renaissance literature in the context of modern media.

Jeffrey R. Wilson is a faculty member in the Writing Program at Harvard University, USA, where he teaches the *Why Shakespeare?* section of the university's first-year writing course. Focused on intersections of Renaissance literature and modern sociology, his work has appeared in academic journals such as *Modern Language Quarterly*, *Genre*, and *College Literature*, and public venues like *National Public Radio*, *Salon*, and MLA's *Profession*.

Shakespeare and *Game of Thrones*

Jeffrey R. Wilson

LONDON AND NEW YORK

First published 2021
by Routledge
2 Park Square, Milton Park, Abingdon, Oxon OX14 4RN

and by Routledge
52 Vanderbilt Avenue, New York, NY 10017

Routledge is an imprint of the Taylor & Francis Group, an informa business

© 2021 Jeffrey R. Wilson

The right of Jeffrey R. Wilson to be identified as author of this work has been asserted by him in accordance with sections 77 and 78 of the Copyright, Designs and Patents Act 1988.

All rights reserved. No part of this book may be reprinted or reproduced or utilised in any form or by any electronic, mechanical, or other means, now known or hereafter invented, including photocopying and recording, or in any information storage or retrieval system, without permission in writing from the publishers.

Trademark notice: Product or corporate names may be trademarks or registered trademarks, and are used only for identification and explanation without intent to infringe.

British Library Cataloguing-in-Publication Data
A catalogue record for this book is available from the British Library

Library of Congress Cataloging-in-Publication Data
Names: Wilson, Jeffrey R. (Jeffrey Robert), 1982– author.
Title: Shakespeare and Game of thrones / Jeffrey R. Wilson.
Description: Abingdon, Oxon; New York, NY: Routledge, 2021. | Includes bibliographical references and index.
Identifiers: LCCN 2020027376 (print) | LCCN 2020027377 (ebook) | ISBN 9780367483920 (hardback) | ISBN 9781003039662 (ebook)
Subjects: LCSH: Game of thrones (Television program) | Martin, George R. R. Song of ice and fire. | Shakespeare, William, 1564–1616—Influence. | History on television. | Literature and history. | Great Britain—History—Wars of the Roses, 1455–1485—Literature and the war.
Classification: LCC PN1992.77.G35 W54 2021 (print) | LCC PN1992.77.G35 (ebook) | DDC 791.45/72—dc23
LC record available at https://lccn.loc.gov/2020027376
LC ebook record available at https://lccn.loc.gov/2020027377

ISBN: 978-0-367-48392-0 (hbk)
ISBN: 978-1-003-03966-2 (ebk)

Typeset in Times New Roman
by codeMantra

For the *Why Shakespeare?* students

Contents

List of figures ix
Acknowledgements x

Introduction 1

1 The Tudor myth 9

2 Martin's Shakespeare 17

3 The Shakespearean slingshot 23

4 Composition history and co(rporate)-authorship 37

5 From true tragedy to historical fantasy 41

6 Comical-tragical-historical-pastoral: mixed genre 45

7 Narrative relief: from comedy to nudity 48

8 Spectacle and success from the medieval church service to CGI 53

9 *Game of Thrones* as Shakespearean performance: interviews with the actors 57

10 External predictability, internal unpredictability 67

11	Eddard as Gloucester: *De Casibus Virorum Illustrium*	69
12	Wars of roses: a literary trope in social life	74
13	The stigmatized protagonist: the tragic model and the heroic model	79
14	Girl power: mimetic feminism and rhetorical misogyny	85
15	Generic bias: gender, race, criticism	92
16	*The Bloody Hand*: intertextual metatheater	101
17	The Targaryen myth	107
18	How George R.R. Martin changed the ending of *Game of Thrones*	110
19	Fandom as IKEA effect	115
	Index	122

Figures

I.1	Mya Lixian Gosling, "Happy 451st Birthday, Shakespeare!" *Good Tickle Brain* (April 23, 2015), https://goodticklebrain.com/home/2015/4/22/happy-451st-birthday-shakespeare	4
1.1	The Tudor myth: a genealogy	11
1.2	The Targaryen myth: a genealogy	14
2.1	"England at the Time of the Conquest," in vol. 1 of Thomas B. Costain, *A History of the Plantagenets* (New York: Doubleday, 1949–62), front matter	18
3.1	Shakespeare on screen, 1898–2014, showing relative popularity	25
3.2	Shakespeare on screen, 1915–2014, showing relative popularity	25
9.1	Emilia Clarke as Daenerys Targaryen, on set with her "dragon." Image from Pixomondo, "Game of Thrones Season 4 Making Of," *YouTube* (Jan. 29, 2015), https://www.youtube.com/watch?v=ssJwFjyS7q8	58
11.1	Visual effect of Ned Stark's head on a spike in *Game of Thrones* (1.10)	69
11.2	Visual effect of Richard, Duke of York's head on a spike in *The Hollow Crown: The Wars of the Roses*, dir. Dominic Cooke (BBC, 2016). Episode 2	70
19.1	Shakespeare's first tetralogy: the nested plots	117
19.2	*Game of Thrones*: the nested plots	118

Acknowledgements

I am grateful to the students in our *Why Shakespeare?* class—to whom this book is dedicated—for the pleasure and privilege of working with so many amazing minds over many years. Much of this book grew from classroom conversations during the two years we studied *Game of Thrones* alongside Shakespeare's first tetralogy. I'm especially grateful to several students whose essays prompted and refined certain lines of thought: Harry Fu (Chapter 10), Iman Lavery (Chapter 18), Cinthya Meza (Chapter 12), and Diana Myers (Chapter 13). I also benefitted from conversations and comments on the manuscript from colleagues, including Guillermina Altomonte, Kavita Mudan Finn, Ella Frigyik, Ronan Hatfull, Steve Purcell, Amy Rodgers, Lauren Swiderski (@ShakesOfThrones), Jessica Walker, W.B. Worthen, Rose Wynn (@HollowCrownFans), and Jess Zimmerman. I appreciate support and encouragement from Brooke Carlson, Ambereen Dadabhoy, Marina Gerzic, Peter C. Herman, Thomas Johnson, Maria Devlin McNair, James McNamara, Stephen O'Neill, Daniel Pollack-Pelzner, and Melissa Rohrer. I'm grateful to Julian Glover, Conleth Hill, and Anton Lesser for providing interviews, and to Richard Johnston, Rachael Swanston, and Vena Dacent for facilitating these conversations. Karen Heath and Tom John provided helpful guidance when I was teaching these texts, and Becky Skolnik and Colleen Desrosiers Laude helped create the classrooms where our conversations took place. Polly Dodson shepherded the book through the publication process at Routledge, with key contributions from Zoe Meyer, Fiona Hudson Gabuya, and Manikandan Kuppan.

Game of Thrones and Shakespeare matter to me for the same reason: not for their literary quality, which I don't really know how to judge, but for the conversations they can create, especially those that go beyond academia. I always looked forward to talking about *Game of Thrones* with my barber, Sam McDonald. I especially enjoyed conversations this project allowed in House Wilson: my wonderful parents, Tom and Jan, and Chris Wilson and Anna Allen. I always feel so much love and support from House Dolan, including the Jareczes, Tiexieras, and Tighes. Conversations with my kids, Liam and Margaret, help me activate the ethics of the analytical work we do in academia. And my spouse, Allison, has been the perfect partner to build a life with, without whom this project wouldn't have been possible.

Introduction

Warrior queens, child kings, royal bastards, scheming uncles, feuding families, shifting allegiances, usurpation, decapitation, incest, toxic masculinity, toxic monarchy, a sprawling cast of characters, genealogical charts, ardent fans, a global literary event—take Shakespeare, add dragons, zombies, naked people, and corporate interests, take away the verse, and you get *Game of Thrones*.

Widely known for these naked people and magic dragons, the hit HBO series *Game of Thrones*, adapted from George R.R. Martin's fantasy novels, *A Song of Ice and Fire*, drew its central storyline from historical source material in the Wars of the Roses, a bloody fifteenth-century civil war among feuding noble families in England.[1] The Wars of the Roses involved the House of Lancaster (whose emblem was the red rose) and the House of York (the white) battling for the English crown amidst competing claims to the proper line of hereditary succession. Yorks unseated Lancasters, then were unseated by the upstart House of Tudor, inaugurating a period of peace and prosperity in England that included the reigns of Henry VIII and his daughter, Elizabeth I. The central parallel in *A Song of Ice and Fire* involves the Starks as the Yorks, the Lannisters as the Lancasters, and the Targaryens as the Tudors, as detailed in books and websites recounting "the history behind *Game of Thrones*."[2] Even the cadence of Martin's title, *A Song of Ice and Fire*, recalls the Wars of the Roses, the ice pointing to the white rose, the fire to the red. In the author's own words from 1998:

> The Wars of the Roses have always fascinated me, and certainly did influence *A Song of Ice and Fire*, but there's really no one-for-one character-for-character correspondence. I like to use history

to flavor my fantasy, to add texture and versimillitude, but simply rewriting history with the names changed has no appeal for me. I prefer to reimagine it all, and take it in new and unexpected directions.[3]

Four hundred years before Martin gave the Tudors dragons, another famous writer told the story of the Wars of the Roses in a very different way. Written in collaboration with other authors in the early 1590s, William Shakespeare's dramatization of the Wars of the Roses comprises his "first tetralogy"—his first set of four plays that tell a single story (Shakespeare's "second tetralogy" was composed later in the 1590s as a prequel of sorts, depicting the English history that led up to the Wars of the Roses).[4] Martin clearly knew the Wars of the Roses, but was he also familiar with and influenced by Shakespeare's plays about them?

Martin—who taught English and Journalism for three years at Clarke College in Dubuque, Iowa in the late 1970s[5]—is certainly familiar with Shakespeare in general. Statements on his website include references to *Julius Caesar* ("Shakespeare wrote that Brutus was 'the noblest Roman of them all'"), *Romeo and Juliet* ("Shakespeare had to kill Mercutio because he was taking over play"), and *Richard III* ("Shakespeare's Richard is a great character, even if he doesn't have much to do with the real historical Richard").[6] Martin put lines from Shakespeare's *Sonnets* into CBS's *Beauty and the Beast* (1987–90), where he was a staff writer.[7] His favorite sci-fi movie is *Forbidden Planet*, which he notes is an adaptation of *The Tempest*.[8] He quotes *Julius Caesar* in interviews ("The evil that men do lives after them; / The good is oft interrèd with their bones" [3.2.67–68]).[9] And he cites Shakespeare when asked about the horrors of war:

> Shakespeare refers to it, in those great scenes in *Henry V*, where King Hal is walking among the men, before the Battle of Agincourt, and he hears the men complaining. "Well, I hope his cause is just, because a lot of us are going to die to make him king of France."[10]

Martin even characterizes his very first publication as a shot at Shakespeare: "It was *Fantastic Four* #17. It was a letter. It said something like, 'Stan Lee, better than Shakespeare'."[11] In keeping with this comment, Martin places Shakespeare in a circle of his three greatest influences: "Maybe Stan Lee is the greatest literary influence on me, even more than Shakespeare or Tolkien."[12] Martin even aligned his approach to adapting the Wars of the Roses with Shakespeare, when asked about his imagination:

> I don't know if I'd ever claim it's enormously original. You look at Shakespeare, who borrowed all of his plots. In *A Song of Ice and Fire*, I take stuff from the Wars of the Roses and other fantasy things, and all these things work around in my head and somehow they jell into what I hope is uniquely my own.[13]

Shakespeare scholars such as Amy Rodgers have identified allusions to specific Shakespearean moments: Robert Baratheon gored by a boar during a hunting accident recalls Shakespeare's *Venus and Adonis*; one of Martin's characters saying "Heavy is the head that wears the crown" is almost a direct quotation of Shakespeare's Henry IV saying "Uneasy lies the head that wears a crown" (*2 Henry IV*, 3.1.31); Martin's Varys musing "And who would mourn poor Varys then?" is an ironic twist on Antony's lamentation for Caesar, "What cause withholds you, then, to mourn for him?" (*Julius Caesar*, 3.2.95); the noble bastard Jon Snow parallels the Bastard in Shakespeare's *King John*; and, according to Rodgers, "Winterfell's set is a ringer for Macbeth's stronghold in Roman Polanski's 1971 adaptation."[14] Fans in online forums have found additional connections: allusions to three Shakespearean tragedies (*King Lear*, *Hamlet*, and *Othello*) in a single chapter (*GoT*, Daenerys IX); the army of moving trees attacking Asha Greyjoy resembling the Birnam Wood in *Macbeth*; the ambitious witch-fueled Stannis Baratheon as an echo of Macbeth; Jon Snow's death and Julius Caesar's; the Thyestean feast in *Titus Andronicus* and the Frey pies; and *The Bloody Hand*, a play-within-the-novel from the "Mercy" chapter of *The Winds of Winter*, which echoes *Richard III* and *Hamlet*.[15] Blog posts propose more parallels, including Petyr Baelish as Iago and Robert Baratheon as Falstaff.[16] Actors in the show have made analogies, as when Gwendoline Christie glossed Jaime Lannister's road trip with Brienne: "There is this thing in Shakespeare that when people go into the woods, it's often symbolic of confusion."[17] And, shifting from specific allusions to thematic echoes, scholars such as Jessica Walker have emphasized similar ways of remembering the past in Shakespeare's first tetralogy and *A Song of Ice and Fire*:

> The parallel historiographies in question include the role of Providence, which surfaces in *A Song of Ice and Fire* through the act of prophecies and portents; Fortune's Wheel, symbolized in Martin's

4 *Introduction*

work through the unusual passage of seasons in his world and his use of rise-and-fall imagery; the related but distinct concept of *memento mori* or *valar morghulis*, which reminds the reader of the inevitability of death; and the use of proto-Gothic imagery to underscore a cyclical interpretation of history, embodied here by the forces of ice and fire.[18]

Turning from texts to receptions, Dan Venning argues that the Shakespearean ancestry of *Game of Thrones* helps the show, like Shakespeare's plays and their afterlives, bridge highbrow and lowbrow culture—professional literary critics and pop-culture fans.[19]

For instance, the artist Mya Gosling, who draws "the world's foremost (and possibly only) stick-figure Shakespeare webcomic," *Good Tickle Brain*, celebrated Shakespeare's birthday in 2015 with a comic suggesting the only difference between Shakespeare and *Game of Thrones* is dragons (see Figure I.1).[20] Fans have written Shakespeare and *Game of Thrones* mash-ups, one in 2016 imagining how showrunners Benioff and Weiss would butcher *Much Ado about Nothing* ("Hero falls in love with Don John because she is a stupid young woman and has no foresight").[21] Perhaps the most amusing connection to

Figure I.1 Mya Lixian Gosling, "Happy 451st Birthday, Shakespeare!" *Good Tickle Brain* (April 23, 2015), https://goodticklebrain.com/home/2015/4/22/happy-451st-birthday-shakespeare.

Introduction   5

Shakespeare came in "George R.R. Martin's Open Letter About the Deaths in *Game of Thrones*," written in 2014 in response to online chatter about his habit of killing off main characters:

> Allow me to pose this question to you—how many of you have heard of **William GODDAMN Shakespeare**? In case you illiterate shitlords aren't familiar, he's the most famous, accomplished, well-known author in human history—and a guy who would kill off characters in insanely brutal ways like it was nothing ALL OF THE GODDAMN TIME.[22]

The letter continues with a series of comparisons ("Let's just say *MacBeth* makes the Red Wedding look like a bridal shower"). The massive attention the letter received online forced Martin to publicly clarify that it wasn't actually written by him (it was a satirical essay by a blogger named Andrew Bridgman).[23]

The missing piece in all these intersections of Shakespeare and Martin is sustained attention on the most obvious and meaningful connection between the two authors: the shared source material of the first tetralogy and *A Song of Ice and Fire* in the Wars of the Roses. This book asks what someone who knows Shakespeare's first tetralogy (as opposed to the history of the Wars of the Roses more generally) understands about *A Song of Ice and Fire* (the books) and *Game of Thrones* (the show) that someone unfamiliar with the Shakespearean texts might miss. In keeping with the expansive and episodic nature of the texts under consideration, there is not a single story told in this book but, rather, a series of interweaving observations. My hope is that, taken together, these vignettes reveal Martin's debt to the literary strategies and achievements in Shakespeare's first tetralogy as distinct from Martin's use of the history of the Wars of the Roses as source material. These comparisons also illuminate how Shakespeare and Martin worked as authors and the conditions of literary production during the different eras in which they wrote. I include interviews with some *Game of Thrones* actors, and some reflections on how *Game of Thrones* fits into the history of Shakespearean adaptation. And in the end, I suggest the comparison with Shakespeare helps us understand how Martin changed the ending of *Game of Thrones*, and why fans love these texts so much.

Because its narrative is long and complex, *Game of Thrones* starts with a title sequence mapping out the locations of the narrative. I'll follow suit here with a map of the disciplinary locations of the book that follows. After Chapter 1 surveys the relevant historical

6 *Introduction*

background, Chapter 2 delivers the book's main argument, laying out a case for Shakespeare's powerful yet indirect presence in *Game of Thrones*, drawing upon the discourse on Martin's medievalism led by scholars such as Shiloh Carroll and Kavita Mudan Finn. Chapter 3 invokes Adaptation Studies to analyze *Game of Thrones* as what Kevin Wetmore and Adam Hansen call a "Shakespearean echo," viewing George R.R. Martin as what Valerie M. Fazel and Louise Geddes call a "Shakespeare user." Authorship Studies inform Chapter 4 (about collaboration). In the first half of the book, Chapters 4–9 are comparative, examining parallels and divergences, invoking disciplines such as Film and Television Studies (Chapters 3, 4, 7, and 8), Genre Studies (Chapters 5 and 6), Performance Studies (Chapter 9), and Audience Studies (Chapter 10). The second half of the book shifts from a comparative to a historicist methodology, Chapters 11–19 asking how Martin used Shakespeare as a source, and how their different time periods influenced their shared tropes, motifs, devices, characters, and plots. These readings are interdisciplinary: Political Science informs Chapters 12 and 17; Sociology appears in Chapters 13, 14, and 19; and Gender Studies arise in Chapters 14 and 15. Theory from these disciplines is used to explicate our literary texts, but Chapter 12 offers an example of "Shakespeare for Theory" where literature is not the recipient of theory in the service of exegesis but the origin of new theory then offered to other disciplines. The final third of the book also spotlights questions of reception. Chapter 15 looks at criticism on race and gender in Shakespeare and Martin's texts, building on conversations begun by Carroll, Finn, Helen Young, and Mat Hardy, among others. Chapter 18 shows Martin cycling the various possible endings of *A Song of Ice and Fire* through Shakespeare. And Chapter 19 concludes the book from the vantage of Fan Studies.

Notes

1 References to the novel series are to George R.R. Martin, *A Song of Ice and Fire* (New York: Bantam, 1996-Press) and are cited in-text by abbreviated volume title: *GoT* = *A Game of Thrones* (1996), *CoK* = *A Clash of Kings* (1999), *SoS* = *A Storm of Swords* (2000), *FfC* = *A Feast for Crows* (2005), *DwD* = *A Dance with Dragons* (2011). References to David Benioff and D.B. Weiss's television show *Game of Thrones* (HBO, 2011-Press) are cited in-text by season and episode.
2 See Jamie Adair, *History behind Game of Thrones*, http://history-behind-game-of-thrones.com. For more scholarly examinations, see Carolyne Larrington, *Winter Is Coming: The Medieval World of Game of Thrones* (London: I.B. Tauris, 2016); *Game of Thrones versus History: Written in Blood*, ed. Brian Pavlac (Hoboken: Wiley Blackwell, 2017); Ayelet Haimson

Lushkov, *You Win or You Die: The Ancient World of Game of Thrones* (London: Bloomsbury, 2017); Ken Mondschein, *Game of Thrones and the Medieval Art of War* (Jefferson: McFarland, 2017); Carol Parrish Jamison, *Chivalry in Westeros: The Knightly Code of A Song of Ice and Fire* (Jefferson: McFarland, 2018); David C. Weinczok, *The History Behind Game of Thrones: The North Remembers* (Havertown: Pen & Sword, 2019); and Ed West, *Iron, Fire and Ice: The Real History that Inspired Game of Thrones* (New York: Skyhorse, 2019).
3. George R.R. Martin, "More Wars of the Roses," in *The Citadel: The Archive of 'A Song of Ice and Fire' Lore* (Nov. 27, 1998), http://www.westeros.org/Citadel/SSM/Entry/950.
4. References to Shakespeare's plays are to *The New Oxford Shakespeare: Modern Critical Edition*, ed. Gary Taylor, John Jowett, Terri Bourus, and Gabriel Egan (Oxford: Oxford University Press, 2016) and are cited in-text by abbreviated play title.
5. Kyle Munson, "Iowa Tie to 'Game of Thrones' Series," *Des Moines Register* (May 20, 2014), https://www.desmoinesregister.com/story/news/local/kyle-munson/2014/05/21/game-thrones-series-ex-iowa-professor-wrote-kyle-munson/2303526/.
6. On *The Citadel: The Archive of A Song of Ice and Fire' Lore*, see "Odyssey Con 2008 (Madison, WI; April 4–6 2008)" (April 6, 2008): http://www.westeros.org/Citadel/SSM/Entry/Odyssey_Con_2008_Madison_WI_April_4_6_20081; "Matters of Honor" (June 19, 2001): http://www.westeros.org/Citadel/SSM/Entry/Matters_of_Honor; and "Producing Valyrian Steel" (March 11, 2001): http://www.westeros.org/Citadel/SSM/Entry/Producing_Valyrian_Steel.
7. Seth Abramovitch, "George R. R. Martin on Writing TV's 'Beauty and the Beast': 'It Was Such a Smart Show'," *The Hollywood Reporter* (March 16, 2017), https://www.hollywoodreporter.com/live-feed/george-r-r-martin-writing-tvs-beauty-beast-was-a-smart-show-986786.
8. Kathy Wang, "Interview with George R.R. Martin," *Feather Factor* (Feb. 15, 2012), https://www.featherfactor.com/2012/02/interview-with-george-r-r-martin.html.
9. Charles Yu, "George R. R. Martin, Fantasy's Reigning King," *The New York Times Style Magazine* (Oct. 15, 2018), https://www.nytimes.com/2018/10/15/t-magazine/george-rr-martin-got-interview.html.
10. Mikal Gilmore, "George R.R. Martin: The Rolling Stone Interview," *Rolling Stone* (April 23, 2014), https://www.rollingstone.com/culture/culture-news/george-r-r-martin-the-rolling-stone-interview-242487/.
11. Andrea Warner, "Fantasy for Non-Fantasy People," *AbeBooks* (2006), https://www.abebooks.com/docs/Fantasy/george-martin.shtml. Martin's letter gushing about *Fantastic Four* doesn't actually mention Shakespeare; see Michael Rothman, "See: 'Game of Thrones' Author George R.R. Martin's Letter to Marvel When He Was 15," *ABC News* (June 20, 2014), https://abcnews.go.com/Entertainment/game-thrones-author-george-rr-martins-letter-marvel/story?id=24218804.
12. Fiona Macdonald, "Who Inspired the Game of Thrones Creator," *BBC* (Oct. 21, 2014), http://www.bbc.com/culture/story/20140826-who-inspired-george-rr-martin.
13. Gilmore, "The Rolling Stone Interview."

8 *Introduction*

14 Amy Rodgers, "History as Echo: Entertainment Historiography from Shakespeare to HBO's *Game of Thrones*," in *Shakespearean Echoes*, ed. Adam Hansen and Kevin J. Wetmore, Jr. (New York: Palgrave Macmillan, 2015): 142–54, quote from 150.
15 See Reddit discussions including glass_table_girl, "Will Daenerys die?" (2016): https://www.reddit.com/r/asoiaf/comments/3cmq0s/will_daenerys_die_spoilers_all/csxdvdy/; Bristol_Aero_Student, "GRRM & Shakespeare" (2015), https://www.reddit.com/r/asoiaf/comments/2hxf3j/spoilers_all_grrm_shakespeare/; and GooseCogens, "Richard III in 'Mercy'" (2015), https://www.reddit.com/r/asoiaf/comments/24mqdu/spoilers_all_richard_iii_in_mercy/#bottom-comments. And see the fan website *Shakespeare of Thrones*, whose author Lauren Swiderski, gave the presentation "The Influence of Shakespeare in *A Song of Ice and Fire* and *Game of Thrones*," at the second annual *Con of Thrones* in Dallas, TX (May 2018), as well as her essay, "Stannis Baratheon: Macbeth Revisited," *Shakespeare of Thrones* (May 18, 2018), https://shakespeareofthrones.com/2018/05/18/stannis-baratheon-macbeth-revisited/.
16 See, for example, Jun Yan, "Shakespeare's Shadow on *Game of Thrones*: The Art of Villainy," *History Behind Game of Thrones* (Oct. 23, 2014), http://history-behind-game-of-thrones.com/warofroses/richardiii/villainy; Andrew Lanham, "Shakespearean Echoes: Game of Thrones as History Play," *The Millions* (July 10, 2017), https://themillions.com/2017/07/shakespearean-echoes-game-thrones-history-play.html; and Lisa Waugh, "Everything *Game of Thrones* Stole from Shakespeare," *Ranker* (n.d.), https://www.ranker.com/list/things-game-of-thrones-took-from-shakespeare/lisa-waugh.
17 Gwendoline Christie, quoted in C.A. Taylor, *Inside HBO's Game of Thrones II: Seasons 3 & 4* (San Francisco: Chronicle Books, 2014), 135.
18 Jessica Walker, "'Just Songs in the End': Historical Discourses in Shakespeare and Martin," in *Mastering the Game of Thrones: Essays on George R.R. Martin's A Song of Ice and Fire*, ed. Jes Battis and Susan Johnston (Jefferson: McFarland, 2015), 75.
19 Dan Venning, "*Game of Thrones* as *Gesamtkunstwerk*: Adapting Shakespeare and Wagner," in *Vying for the Iron Throne: Essays on Power, Gender, Death, and Performance in HBO's Game of Thrones*, ed. Lindsey Mantoan and Sara Brady (Jefferson: McFarland, 2018): 148–58.
20 Mya Lixian Gosling, "About," *Good Tickle Brain*, https://goodticklebrain.squarespace.com/about/.
21 Zach, "Benioff and Weiss Adapt Shakespeare's Much Ado about Nothing," *The Fandomentals* (March 8, 2016), https://www.thefandomentals.com/dd-adapt-shakespeare-much-ado-nothing/.
22 Andrew Bridgman, "George R.R. Martin's Open Letter about the Deaths in Game of Thrones," *Dorkly* (June 5, 2014): http://www.dorkly.com/post/63864/george-rr-martins-open-letter-about-the-deaths-in-game-of-thrones.
23 Andrew Bridgman, "We Pranked the Internet So Hard That George RR Martin Had To Get Involved," *Dorkly* (April 11, 2016), http://www.dorkly.com/post/77792/we-pranked-the-internet-so-hard-that-george-rr-martin-had-to-get-involved.

1 The Tudor myth

This briskly telescoped history of medieval English royalty shows how many of the same themes pop up in *Game of Thrones*: internal civil war and external foreign war, women in politics, church versus state, royal authority versus people's rights, counselor in-fighting, the line of succession, the child king, and monarchy versus meritocracy, among others.[1]

The most important year in English history is 1066. King Edward the Confessor died with no children. After a skirmish among nobles, a bastard from Normandy (Northern France) was crowned King of England: William the Conqueror is famous for bringing high-class French culture to low-class England. And the addition of William's lands in Normandy to the English territory created a centuries-long territorial dispute between England and France.

All politics was family politics. William the Conqueror's granddaughter, Empress Matilda (1102–67), laid claim to the crown in 1141, activating the question of women in politics early in England's royal history. Matilda married a teenage Frenchman with golden red hair named Geoffrey, nicknamed Plantagenet (referring to the yellow flower of the broom shrub, or *planta genista*). The long line of monarchs descending from Matilda and Geoffrey is called the Plantagenet dynasty.

Matilda's son, Henry II (1133–89), became the first Plantagenet king in 1154. His wife, Eleanor of Aquitaine, had divorced King Louis of France to marry Henry. With their lands combined, Henry and Eleanor controlled England and half of France, marking the start of the Angevin empire where Kings of England claimed French lands. Henry is most famous for ordering the death of his good friend, Thomas a Becket. The two were playboys in their youths, so Henry named Becket Archbishop of Canterbury to keep the power of the church in check. Becket turned on Henry and asserted the power of the church over the state, asking a famous question—"Will no one rid me of this meddlesome priest?"—which was understood to be a command, as dramatized in T.S. Eliot's *Murder in the Cathedral* (1935) and quoted in, for example, former CIA director James Comey's testimony about US President Donald Trump's corruption.[2] After Becket's murder, the pope declared him a saint, Henry later performing a public walk of atonement to Canterbury Cathedral, throwing himself down on the church steps, allowing the clergy to beat him.

Henry's crown was taken from him in 1189 by one of his sons, Richard I (1157–99), known as Richard the Lionheart. Richard fancied himself a hero, as he is portrayed in the Robin Hood stories. He spent most of his time on crusades in the holy land. Richard's younger brother, King John, is the villain in the Robin Hood stories. That's because John killed one of his nephews, Arthur, whom the French saw as the rightful heir. Wicked uncles unwilling to submit to their nephews are all over medieval English history. John was also seen as a villain—from the royal perspective—because he was forced by barons to sign the Magna Carta in 1215, which limited the power of the king, a precursor to modern political ideas of people's rights. Most of all, John was remembered unfavorably because, after the death of Arthur, the French drove him and his English forces out of most of the land in France. This marked the end of the Angevin empire. The future was grim for the Plantagenets.

John's son, Henry III (1207–72), crowned in 1216 when he was nine years old, is famous for building Westminster Abbey. In the wake of the Magna Carta, he created Parliament (further raising issues about royal authority versus people's rights). In an episode called the Mad Parliament, Henry's brother-in-law, a baron named Simon du Monfrey, even captured Henry and ruled the country for a while (sparking questions about who should rule, the monarch born into power or the representative of the people who most merits power). The throne passed to Henry's son, Edward I (1239–1307)—an autocrat, cruel, even to his own children—and then to his son, Edward II (1284–1327). Edward II fell in love with one of his advisors, Pierce Gaveston, who wore the queen's jewelry to Edward's coronation. Feuding nobles killed Gaveston, leaving Edward devastated. Edward's wife, Queen Isabella, rebelled against him and had him deposed. Legend has it that she eventually had Edward killed in a way that wouldn't leave any marks of murder: he was stabbed through the anus with a red-hot poker. Isabella put her and Edward's son on the throne—Edward III (1312–77), crowned in 1327. Like any good English king, Edward III went to war with France, increasing some of the lands lost at the end of the Angevin empire, losing them again by the end of his reign.

The Tudor myth 11

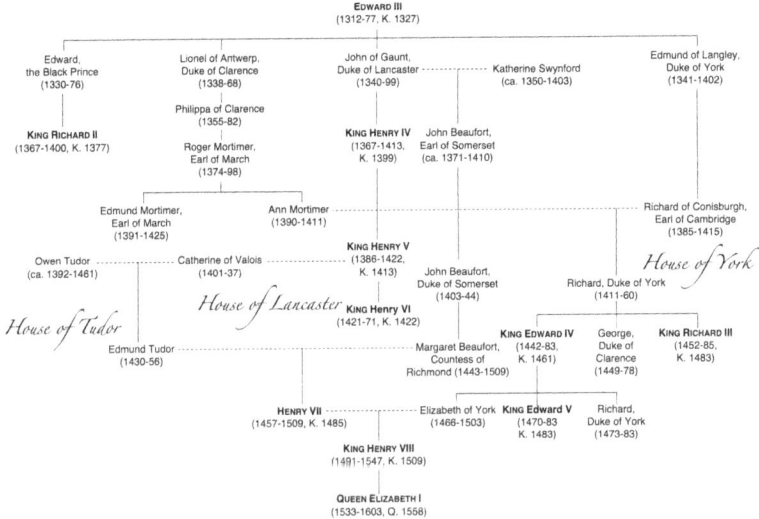

Figure 1.1 The Tudor myth: a genealogy.

Here's where things heat up as we look toward *Game of Thrones*, and where we'll slow down. That's because Martin did not adapt an objective historical account of the Wars of the Roses as much as he adapted the heavily politicized version memorably depicted in Shakespeare's history plays, dubbed "the Tudor myth" by Shakespeare scholar E.M.W. Tillyard.[3] As depicted in Figure 1.1, the Tudor myth began when Edward III's eldest son and heir, Edward the Black Prince, died in 1376, one year before his father died in 1377. The line of royal succession passed to the eldest son's eldest son, the Black Prince's ten-year-old child, Richard II (1367–1400). Petulant, entitled, impulsive, weak, Joffrey-like, Richard's inefficiency as a governor brought to the surface the tension in medieval English politics between traditionalists arguing for hereditary monarchy and innovators sympathetic to meritocracy: the problem of the child king always creates the problem of counselor in-fighting. Richard's uncle, John of Gaunt, Duke of Lancaster, another of Edward III's sons, believing he and his family could run the country better than Richard, organized a rebellion that deposed Richard and placed Gaunt's son, Henry IV (1367–1413), on the throne in 1399. Henry's son, Henry V (1386–1422), became king in 1413, his reign shifting attention from civil war to foreign war. Starting with the Battle of Agincourt, Henry V retook lands in Northern

12 The Tudor myth

France, becoming a national hero. But those lands were lost again during the reign of his son, Henry VI (1421–71), as Shakespeare memorably captured in the "fatal prophecy ... That 'Henry born at Monmouth should win all, / And Henry born at Windsor should lose all'" (*1 Henry VI*, 3.1.194–98).

Henry VI was an infant when crowned in 1422 after his father died at a young age. Again, the child king; again, counselor in-fighting, though a common enemy in the foreign war against France unified the English houses for a time, staving off civil war. English forces defeated the fierce French female warrior Joan of Arc, who was burned at the stake, but England lost most of its land in France. Attention turned back from foreign to civil war. Henry married a French queen, Margaret of Anjou, who came with no dowry, causing discord among Henry's advisors. In Shakespeare's version, Margaret has a secret love affair with one of her husband's closest allies, the Duke of Suffolk, and Humphrey, Duke of Gloucester—the king's noble uncle—is churned up in the chaos.

Factions emerged in England's royal families, the tension between monarchy and meritocracy resurfacing. Henry, Margaret, their son Prince Edward, and the House of Lancaster (the descendants of John of Gaunt) argued in favor of monarchy and a hereditary line of succession. They were opposed by the House of York (the descendants of Edmund of Langley, Duke of York, the younger brother of Edward the Black Prince and John of Gaunt). Richard, Duke of York made a tenuous claim to the throne, arguing that the entire Lancastrian line was illegitimate due to the illegal rebellion of Henry IV against Richard II, but the York case was really based in meritocracy: they only seriously advanced the Duke of York's claim to the throne when it became obvious that the weak Henry VI was running the nation into the ground. "This brawl," in Shakespeare's words, "Shall send between the red rose and the white / A thousand souls to death and deadly night" (*1 Henry VI*, 2.4.124–27).

Under pressure from the York faction, Henry VI named Richard, Duke of York his successor, disinheriting Prince Edward and really pissing off Queen Margaret. As the Wars of the Roses erupted, Henry became the subordinate member of his marriage, Margaret a political power-broker (think Cersei) and Lancastrian military leader (think Daenerys). She defeated Richard of York—his head Eddarded on a spike—but York's children took up the family's cause, eventually unseating Henry VI. In 1461, the eldest York brother became King Edward IV (1442–83), but further civil war ensued. There was internal tension within the York family because Edward pulled a Robb Stark and reneged on his promise to marry Lady Bona of France in a politically advantageous union, choosing instead to follow his heart and marry Elizabeth Woodville, a landless English widow. That internal feud within the York family spilled over into the external feud with the Lancasters. Edward's younger brother George, Duke of Clarence, defected to the Lancastrian side; he later came back to the Yorks. The Earl of Warwick, another powerful Yorkist who helped seat Edward IV, also defected, marrying his daughter, Anne Neville, to Henry VI's son Prince Edward, earning Warwick the title of "the kingmaker." Henry VI won back the crown but, like Aerys Targaryen, deteriorated into madness.

According to Shakespeare, if you're Edward and George's youngest brother—Richard, Duke of Gloucester, the youngest living son of Richard, Duke of York—and you yourself want to be king, there's only one option: kill everyone. That's the man who becomes Shakespeare's Richard III. First, in Shakespeare's version, Richard and his brothers kill Prince Edward, Henry VI's heir. Then, Richard kills Henry VI and marries Prince Edward's widow, Anne Neville. With Edward IV back on the throne, Richard next kills his older brother, George. After Edward dies, Richard kills Edward's son, crowned King Edward V in 1483, as well as the next in the line of royal succession, King Edward's younger brother Richard (these are the "princes in the tower"). Only with all these royal claimants out of the way could Richard III become king, which he did in 1483.

The centerpiece of the Tudor myth is the notion that Richard III—a demonic villain whose physical deformity symbolized an evil soul and the generations of political chaos plaguing England ever since Henry IV broke the hereditary line of royal succession in his rebellion against a divinely placed Richard II—was defeated in 1485 at the Battle of Bosworth by Henry Tudor, a young Welsh earl who, on his father's side, was the grandson of Owen Tudor (who secretly married Catherine of Valois, the widow of Henry V) and, on his mother's side, was the great-great-grandson of John of Gaunt and his mistress (whose illegitimate children, born out of wedlock, had been legitimized during the reign of Richard II), giving the young Henry Tudor a tenuous claim, shrouded in secret marriages and bastard births, to be the last surviving Lancaster. Shakespeare even had his Henry VI, all the way back in the midst of the Wars of the Roses, invoke "divining thoughts" to make Henry Tudor the prince who was promised: "This pretty lad will prove our country's bliss" (*3 Henry VI*, 4.7.70–71). Riding under the Welsh symbol of the red dragon, Shakespeare's Henry Tudor prays to that same providence just before his battle against Richard III, calling himself God's "captain" and his army God's "ministers of chastisement" (*Richard III*, 5.4.88–93). After defeating Richard III in a war

14 *The Tudor myth*

Shakespeare presents as one of good versus evil, Henry Tudor became King Henry VII. He brought an end to the feud between Lancasters and Yorks, and decades of civil war, by marrying Edward IV's daughter, Princess Elizabeth of York. That's how Shakespeare's first tetralogy ends, with a mythologized Henry Tudor declaring providential control over the end to the Wars of the Roses and a return to order in the House of Tudor: "We will unite the white rose and the red. / Smile heaven, upon this fair conjunction, / That long have frowned upon their enmity" (*Richard III*, 5.7.19–21). Presented as God's lieutenant on earth, Henry VII established the Tudor dynasty that would be carried on by his son, Henry VIII, and eventually Henry VIII's daughter, Elizabeth I, who was Queen of England when Shakespeare wrote his plays depicting the Wars of the Roses and the Tudor myth.

The Tudor myth is the basis for the central analogy between *A Song of Ice and Fire* and the Wars of the Roses: *Starks as Yorks, Lannisters as Lancasters,* and *Targaryens as Tudors.* In both cases, noble houses feud for a crown put up for grabs during civil war, resulting in the decimation of the Lan- family; peace only returns to the realm when civil war is ended by the union of someone from the -rk family and someone from the T-family. But the Tudor myth, and specifically Shakespeare's treatment of it in his first tetralogy, provides a number of other parallels that readers love to discover and debate—many charted in Figure 1.2:

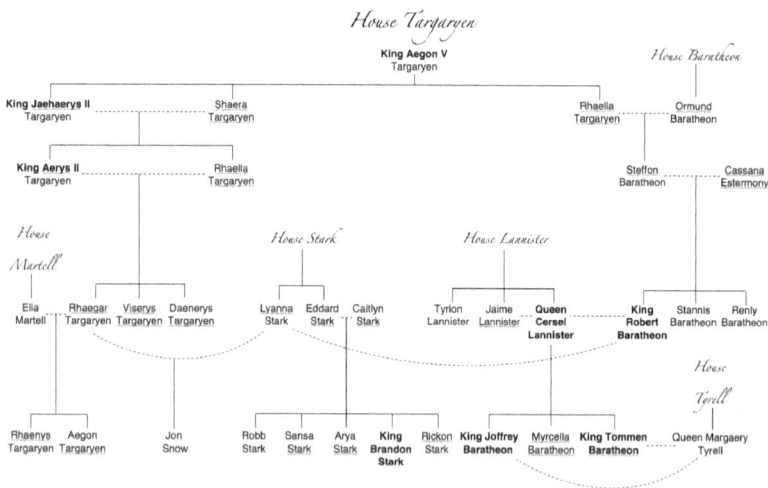

Figure 1.2 The Targaryen myth: a genealogy.

The Tudor myth   15

The Targaryens
- *Aerys II Targaryen as Richard II*: Weak kings deposed by rival households.
- *Aerys II Targaryen as Henry VI*: Kings who went mad toward the ends of their reigns.
- *Daenerys Targaryen as Margaret of Anjou*: Queens from far-away lands, married off with no say in the matter, who become women warriors and seek to rule the mainland.
- *Daenerys Targaryen as Henry VII*: Children hidden away in a far-off land who lay claim to a throne which is placed up for grabs through civil war.

The Baratheons
- *Robert Baratheon as Henry IV*: Members of a noble family, but not in the line of succession, who are placed as kings after rebellions against sitting kings.
- *Robert Baratheon as Edward IV*: Philandering kings who die early.
- *Joffrey Baratheon as Richard II*: Entitled child kings deposed from the throne.
- *Joffrey Baratheon as Edward, Prince of Wales*: Sons of kings killed by their fathers' enemies.
- *Joffrey Baratheon as Edward V*: Young kings assassinated by political rivals.
- *Stannis Baratheon as Richard, Duke of York*: Heads of noble houses who claim the throne is theirs according to the proper line of succession; killed in battle.
- *Stannis Baratheon as Richard III*: Claimants to the throne who accuse the kings in power of being bastards.
- *Renly Baratheon as George, Duke of Clarence*: Killed by their own brothers' attempts to secure the crown for themselves.
- *Renly Baratheon as Richard III*: Stigmatized (as gay, as deformed) members of noble families, low in the line of succession, who ambitiously try to become kings.

The Lannisters
- *Cercei Lannister as Margaret of Anjou*: Queens who take over the role of governor from their weak husbands and display a willingness to exercise extreme cruelty in defense of their royal sons.
- *Cerci and Jamie Lannister as Margaret and Suffolk*: Secret lovers who hide their forbidden affairs from the King and the rest of the realm.
- *Jon Arryn as Humphrey, Duke of Gloucester*: Honorable councilors to the king killed off through the backstabbing of the king's nobles.
- *Tyrion Lannister as Richard III*: Physically deformed youngest brothers in a royal house, with a penchant for irreverence.

16 The Tudor myth

- *Jamie Lannister as Henry IV*: Kingslayers.
- *Tywin Lannister as Warwick*: Kingmakers.

The Starks
- *Eddard Stark as Richard, Duke of York*: Leaders of noble houses which feud with rival houses who hold the crown; killed through the efforts of the matriarch of the rival faction; heads placed on a spike.
- *Eddard Stark as Humphrey, Duke of Gloucester*: Honorable lord protectors killed off through the backstabbing of the king's nobles.
- *Catelyn Stark as Cecily, Duchess of York*: Matriarchs of out-of-power noble families whose husbands are killed by rival houses and whose sons then mount campaigns to become kings.
- *Robb Stark as Edward IV*: Eldest sons in noble but out-of-power houses who, after the deaths of their fathers, take up the quest to claim the throne for themselves; later, heads of houses who marry for love, disrupting plans for political marriages.
- *Sansa Stark as Anne Neville*: Princesses treated as chattel, betrothed to one nobleman after another.
- *Sansa Stark as Margaret of Anjou*: Women beginning as chattel married off to create royal alliances who become political powerbrokers in their own rights.
- *Arya Stark as Joan of Arc*: Women who reject domestic roles and instead become fierce warriors.
- *Jon Snow as Richard III*: Stigmatized (as deformed, as bastard) members of noble families far down in the line of succession.
- *Jon Snow as Henry VII*: The child with a hidden birthright to the throne.
- *Jon Snow as Henry VIII*: Children whose parentage draws from both sides of the rival families in the civil war, making them unions of warring factions.

Notes

1 Facts and dates in this history are drawn from John Cannon and Ralph Griffiths, *The Oxford Illustrated History of the British Monarchy* (Oxford: Oxford University Press, 1988).
2 See Sara Lipton, "Trump's Meddlesome Priest," *New York Times* (June 8, 2017), https://www.nytimes.com/2017/06/08/opinion/meddlesome-priest-comey-trump.html.
3 See E.M.W. Tillyard, *Shakespeare's History Plays* (London: Chatto & Windus, 1944). For up-to-date accounts of the contentious question of Shakespeare's subscription to the Tudor myth, see Neema Parvini, "Shakespeare's Historical and Political Thought in Context," in *Shakespeare's History Plays* (Edinburgh: Edinburgh University Press, 2012), 84–121; Dan Breen, "Shakespeare and History Writing," *Literature Compass* 14.1 (2017): e12376.

2 Martin's Shakespeare

Is the relationship between Shakespeare's first tetralogy and *Game of Thrones* a case of analogy or influence? Is it two authors responding independently to shared source material—sometimes there are parallels, sometimes divergences? Or was Martin aware of, influenced by, and responding to Shakespeare's text as something independent of the history of the Wars of the Roses? Is there evidence that Martin directly engaged with Shakespeare's first tetralogy?

Much of Shakespeare's influence on Martin is indirect, one step removed via Shakespeare's influence on the two main genres *Game of Thrones* draws upon: fantasy literature and historical fiction.[1] Like most fantasy writers, Martin is a devotee of *The Lord of the Rings*. Despite J.R.R. Tolkien's somewhat hostile attitude toward Shakespeare, scholars have identified a number of generic similarities between Shakespearean drama and fantasy literature.[2] Shakespeare's presence in *A Song of Ice and Fire* is often an echo of an echo just as Shakespeare, thanks to his prominence in the English literary tradition, can be felt in many modern texts, even when the author is not consciously trying to be Shakespearean. For instance, the phrase "the Wars of the Roses" wasn't used to describe this conflict until the nineteenth century, after the canonization of Shakespeare and his histories, which make much of the rose imagery. The sources of Martin's knowledge of the Wars of the Roses are not totally clear, although he has singled out "Thomas B. Costain's monumental (and wonderfully entertaining) four-volume history of the Plantagenets."[3] Costain's collection starts with a map of "England at the Time of the Conquest" (Figure 2.1), which, given the exactness of correspondence, is probably the most direct model for the maps of Westeros at the beginning of the *Song of Ice and Fire* books.

Martin is a voracious reader with a large library (he bought a second house across the street from his home in New Mexico to hold

Figure 2.1 "England at the Time of the Conquest," in vol. 1 of Thomas B. Costain, *A History of the Plantagenets* (New York: Doubleday, 1949–62), front matter.

his many books).[4] Instead of academic research, he prefers popular histories and historical fiction, both discourses heavily influenced by Shakespeare.[5] Like many nineteenth- and twentieth-century royal histories, Costain was openly hostile to Shakespeare, dismissive of the playwright's unhistorical embellishments. Yet Costain still structured his narrative around the Tudor myth codified by Shakespeare: the final volume in Costain's series starts with the birth of Richard II and ends with the death of Richard III. From this vantage, Shakespeare did not directly influence Martin as much as Shakespeare's account of the Wars of the Roses significantly influenced the genres that significantly influenced Martin once he decided to blend epic fantasy and historical fiction together in a tale taking its major cues from the Wars of the Roses—raising complicated questions about Martin's "medievalism."

Tom Shippey defines *medievalism* as "any post-medieval attempt to re-imagine the Middle Ages, or some aspect of the Middle Ages, for the modern world."[6] A related term, *neomedievalism*, has many different meanings. One, voiced by Karl Fugelso, is "interpretations of interpretations of the Middle Ages."[7] Shiloh Carroll explains that

> contemporary understanding of the Middle Ages is heavily influenced by both Renaissance thinkers, particularly Petrarch, who referred to the period as the "Dark Ages" and saw it as a regression from the Classical era, and by the Victorians, who romanticized the Middle Ages as a time of unity and chivalry.[8]

The Victorians imagined the Middle Ages as a pre-industrial golden age with white castles and blond princesses. With *Game of Thrones*, Martin sought to counter this "Disneyland Middle Ages" with something more authentic.[9] Yet *Game of Thrones* has its own neomedievalism. It is "a simulacrum of the medieval—neither an original nor the copy of an original," says Richard Utz—it is a copy of a copy.[10] "[Martin] is not using sources written down during the Middle Ages," Kavita Mudan Finn explains. "He is instead using modern interpretations of those sources."[11] As Carroll and Finn have argued, despite Martin's appeal to authenticity, *Game of Thrones* gives a vague image of the Middle Ages that is both historically inaccurate (because it relies on nineteenth- and twentieth-century histories) and politically offensive (because it repeats the tropes of those outdated histories, especially the ethno- and androcentrism of the Victorian image of the Middle Ages that more recent scholarship has disputed).

Whereas Martin's medievalism claims historical accuracy yet rests on already inaccurate mediations of the Middle Ages from the nineteenth and twentieth centuries—both historical and fictional—those medievalisms themselves derive from the already mythologized medieval world represented by Shakespeare. As Carol Jamison points out, creating a fictional medieval past to represent concerns of the present is something that happens in medieval literature itself.[12] And Deanne Williams and Mike Rodman Jones have illustrated a swath of "early modern medievalisms."[13] Shakespeare certainly had his own (neo)medievalism.[14] Williams reads Chaucer in *Cymbeline* as a "Shakespearean medievalism" that is "fundamentally anachronic, resisting the paradigms of periodization, and bringing together elements of the classical and medieval past, and Shakespeare's present."[15] Helen Cooper calls Shakespeare's *Pericles* "a foundational work of medievalism," even the "invention of medievalism."[16] In his history plays, Shakespeare was not just drawing upon the medieval past; he was drawing upon newer interpretations of the Middle Ages and creating his own image of that era. Shakespeare's history plays show the early-modern origins of medievalism. Martin's medievalism derives from a Victorian medievalism that derives from a Shakespearean medievalism.

At the same time, Martin's engagement with Shakespeare was mediated by modern medieval history that was itself mediated by Shakespeare. "From the late 1590s onward," Philip Schwyzer writes, "There is hardly a poetic or dramatic text dealing with Richard III that does not reflect the influence of Shakespeare on the level of characterization, plot, verbal detail, or—in most cases—all three."[17] Propelled by the popularity of Shakespeare's history plays on English stages in the seventeenth, eighteenth, and nineteenth centuries, as well as the canonization of Shakespeare as England's national treasure, the Tudor myth structuring Shakespeare's first tetralogy became the dominant frame for this historical episode.[18] That makes the medievalism of Victorian historians also a case of "early-modernism," which Marina Gerzic and Aidan Norrie define as "the reception, interpretation, or recreation of the early modern period in post-early modern cultures."[19] *Game of Thrones* is a post-modern recreation of a modern recreation of an early-modern recreation, a medievalism of a medievalism thrice removed from the history that is already once removed from truth. And Martin exhibits a "Shakespeareanism" on the model of medievalism—a post-Shakespearean recreation of Shakespeare—as well as a "neoShakespeareanism" on the model of neomedievalism—an interpretation of interpretations of Shakespeare. *Game of Thrones* was deeply influenced by sources deeply influenced by the characterizations, narratives, and literary devices Shakespeare employed to represent the Wars of the Roses. Not only was Shakespeare one of the intermediaries through which

Martin's medievalism accessed the Middle Ages, but Martin accessed Shakespeare through modern intermediaries.

Given this web of indirect influence, I tried contacting Martin to ask about the extent and shape of his engagement with Shakespeare's first tetralogy. Does he go see Shakespeare at the theater? Does he read Shakespeare at home? Has he studied Shakespeare's first tetralogy? Does he read Shakespeare scholarship? Were Shakespeare's history plays on his desk when he was writing *A Song of Ice and Fire*? No response. Thus, the question becomes: can comparative analysis reveal literary influence and authorial intent? Can it reconstruct the shape of Martin's engagement with Shakespeare?

The readings in the second half of this book illustrate parallels and broken parallels that seem to be deliberate enough to allow us to conclude that Martin was aware of and consciously responding to Shakespeare's first tetralogy, understood as a literary phenomenon distinct from the historical phenomenon of the Wars of the Roses. While there is ample circumstantial evidence suggesting Martin directly engaged with Shakespeare's first tetralogy—such as his self-proclaimed love of Shakespeare and his documented direct engagement with Shakespeare's other plays—it seems likely that Martin's engagement with Shakespeare's first tetralogy was, paradoxically, very deep yet indirect. His most extensive source-work was with popular histories and historical fictions that are not Shakespeare's history plays, yet are informed by them. Martin seems to be more influenced by Shakespearean tropes of characterization and narrative than by Shakespeare's actual texts themselves. Those tropes are available in texts influenced by Shakespeare that are not Shakespeare's actual plays.

Notes

1 When identifying these genres as his main influences, Martin added, "Epic Fantasy and Historical Fiction Are Sisters under the Skin" ("Reading Recommendations," on *Not a Blog* [March 13, 2013], https://grrm.livejournal.com/316785.html).
2 See *Tolkien and Shakespeare: Essays on Shared Themes and Language*, ed. Janet Brennan Croft (Jefferson: McFarland, 2007).
3 George R.R. Martin, "FIRE & BLOOD: On The Way," on *Not a Blog* (April 25, 2018), http://georgerrmartin.com/notablog/2018/04/25/fire-blood-on-the-way/, citing Thomas B. Costain, *A History of the Plantagenets*, 4 vol. (New York: Doubleday, 1949–62).
4 Rachel Ray, "From His Medieval Lair in the New Mexico Mountains, George RR Martin Conjures His *Game of Thrones*," *The Telegraph* (April 6, 2016), https://www.telegraph.co.uk/books/authors/from-his-medieval-lair-in-the-new-mexico-mountains-george-rr-mar/.

5 See Paola Pugliatti, *Shakespeare the Historian* (New York: Palgrave Macmillan, 1996); Martha Tuck Rozett, *Constructing a World: Shakespeare's England and the New Historical Fiction* (Albany: State University of New York Press, 2003).
6 Tom Shippey, "Medievalisms and Why They Matter," *Studies in Medievalism* 17 (2009), 52. See also Richard Utz, "Coming to Terms with Medievalism," *European Journal of English Studies* 15.2 (2011): 101–13.
7 Karl Fugelso, "Neomedievalism as Revised Medievalism in *Commedia* Illustrations," *Studies in Medievalism* 22 (2008), 55.
8 Shiloh Carroll, *The Medievalism of A Song of Ice and Fire and Game of Thrones* (Cambridge: DS Brewer, 2018), 9.
9 "John Hodgman interviews George R.R. Martin," *Public Radio International* (Sept. 21, 2011), https://www.pri.org/stories/2011-09-21/john-hodgman-interviews-george-rr-martin.
10 Richard Utz, "'Game of Thrones' Among the Medievalists," *Inside Higher Ed* (July 14, 2017), https://www.insidehighered.com/views/2017/07/14/why-game-thrones-shouldnt-be-used-effort-recruit-future-medievalists-essay.
11 Kavita Mudan Finn, "*Game of Thrones* is Based in History—Outdated History," *The Public Medievalist* (May 16, 2019), https://www.publicmedievalist.com/thrones-outdated-history/.
12 Carol Jamison, "Reading Westeros: George R.R. Martin's Multi-Layered Medievalisms," *Studies in Medievalism* 26 (2017): 131–42.
13 Deanne Williams, "Medievalism in English Renaissance Literature," in *A Companion to Tudor Literature*, ed. Kent A. Cartwright (Oxford: Wiley Blackwell, 2010), 213–27; Mike Rodman Jones, "Early Modern Medievalism," in *The Cambridge Companion to Medievalism*, ed. Louise D'Arcens (Cambridge: Cambridge University Press, 2016), 89–102.
14 See the essays by Patrick Cheney, William Kuskin, Brian Walsh, and Curtis Perry collected in Part II of *Shakespeare and the Middle Ages*, ed. Curtis Perry and John Watkins (Oxford: Oxford University Press, 2009), 103–98.
15 Deanne Williams, "Shakespearean Medievalism and the Limits of Periodization in *Cymbeline*," *Literature Compass* 8.6 (2011), 396.
16 Helen Cooper, "Encountering the Past II: Shakespearean Comedy, Chaucer, and Medievalism," in *The Oxford Handbook of Shakespearean Comedy*, ed. Heather Hirschfeld (Oxford: Oxford University Press, 2018), 60; Helen Cooper, *Shakespeare and the Medieval World* (London: Bloomsbury, 2014), 196.
17 Philip Schwyzer, *Shakespeare and the Remains of Richard III* (Oxford: Oxford University Press, 2013), 208.
18 Keith Dockray, *William Shakespeare, the Wars of the Roses and the Historians* (Stroud: Tempus, 2002).
19 Marina Gerzic and Aidan Norrie, "Introduction: Medievalism and Early-Modernism in Adaptations of the English Past," in *From Medievalism to Early-Modernism: Adapting the English Past*, ed. Marina Gerzic and Aidan Norrie (New York: Routledge, 2018), 3.

3   The Shakespearean slingshot

Game of Thrones does not, like Baz Luhrmann's *William Shakespeare's Romeo and Juliet* (1996), advertise its indebtedness. You do not need to know the Shakespearean original to comprehend the work, as with the recent film *Ophelia* (2018). So how does *Game of Thrones* fit into the tradition of Shakespearean adaptation? And how does it fit into the specific tradition of Shakespeare on television?

For one thing, *Game of Thrones* helps us see the hidden Shakespearean aspect of Peak TV, the term for the era—associated with the rise of streaming television in the second decade of the twenty-first century—featuring a saturation of high-quality programs.[1] Two of the top five shows of the twenty-first century have clear Shakespearean resonances: *Game of Thrones* is related to Shakespeare's first tetralogy, and *House of Cards* (2013–18) is based on *Richard III*. Two other top-ten shows—*Lost* (2004–10) and *Breaking Bad* (2008–13)—exploit Shakespearean moments and themes, though they are not patterned on any of the plays. And other shows, like *Sons of Anarchy* (2008–14, based on *Hamlet*), *Empire* (2015–Press, based on *King Lear*), and *Star-Crossed* (2014, based on *Romeo and Juliet*), start with explicitly Shakespearean conceits, then drift away from them as the shows go on.

Like these other shows, *Game of Thrones* is an example of the Shakespearean slingshot. This term refers to racing, whether NASCAR or cycling. A racer prepares to slingshot off another by positioning him- or herself directly behind the leading racer. The leader faces more wind resistance and must exert enormous energy to maintain speed, while the trailer preserves energy by staying closely behind in the pocket of no wind resistance created by the leader's draft. After drafting for some time, the trailing racer executes a slingshot, usually during a turn when the racer's centrifugal force is strongest. The trailer shoots out from behind the leader, bursting out all that stored-up energy to sprint in front, leaving the racer who once led the way, now exhausted, to trail off into the background. "Shake and bake," as Will Ferrell and John C. Reilly say in *Talladega Nights: The Ballad of Ricky Bobby* (2006).

Modern writers often "Shake(speare) and bake." In a very general sense of the term, the Shakespearean slingshot has long occurred on the level of both individual text and entire discourse. Films like *West Side Story* (1961, based on *Romeo and Juliet*), *Forbidden Planet* (1956, based on *The Tempest*), and *The Lion King* (1994, based on *Hamlet*) draw core plots and characters from Shakespearean texts, yet slingshot out in different directions, as do the recent novels in the Hogarth Shakespeare Series (2015–21). Entire literary movements also leverage Shakespeare's cultural authority for their own purposes. Consider Shakespeare's presence in Restoration drama, where straightforward performances of Shakespearean plays in the 1660s grew first into adaptations (like William Davenant, John Dryden, and Thomas Shadwell's *The Tempest; or, The Enchanted Island* [1674]) and imitations (like John Dryden's *All for Love* [1678], based on *Antony and Cleopatra*), and then into original plays that moved away from the Shakespearean style. There is also Shakespeare's presence in the film industry. As seen in Figure 3.1, a chart of Shakespeare's presence on screens according to the Internet Movie Database, Shakespeare had a huge footprint in early silent film, which used his existing texts and cultural authority to establish itself before slingshoting away from theater into its own organic idiom for film. The same is true for early television. Starting in 1937, when the first major television network was created, Shakespeare's presence on screens came largely in the form of television series and made-for-TV movies, helping to launch the new medium. As Figure 3.2 shows, Shakespeare's presence on screens peaked in 1964, then declined over the next few decades as television developed its own idiom.

Because there are usually corporate interests behind these efforts to capitalize on Shakespeare's cultural caché, they are often dismissed by critics as "bard biz" or "big-time Shakespeare."[2] But Douglas Lanier reminds us that the relationship is mutually exploitative:

> Shakespeare's association with a mass-cultural product, medium, or genre lends that item a moiety of highbrow depth, "universality," authority, continuity with established tradition, or seriousness of purpose, while at the same time the association with mass culture lends Shakespeare street credibility, broad intelligibility, and celebrity.[3]

The Shakespearean slingshot 25

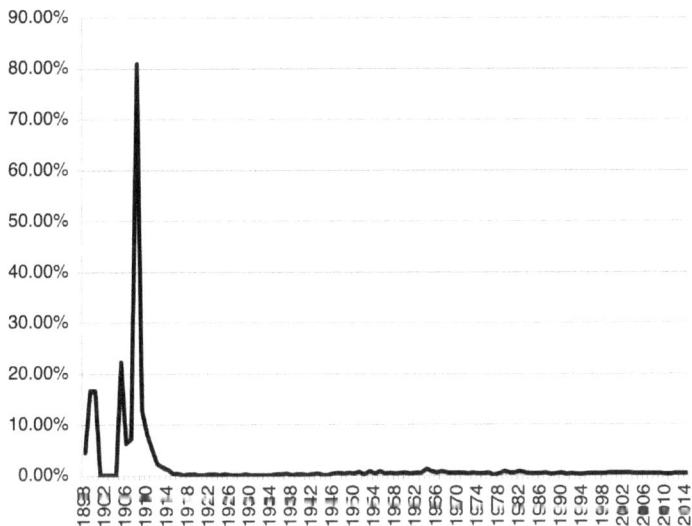

Figure 3.1 Shakespeare on screen, 1898–2014, showing relative popularity.

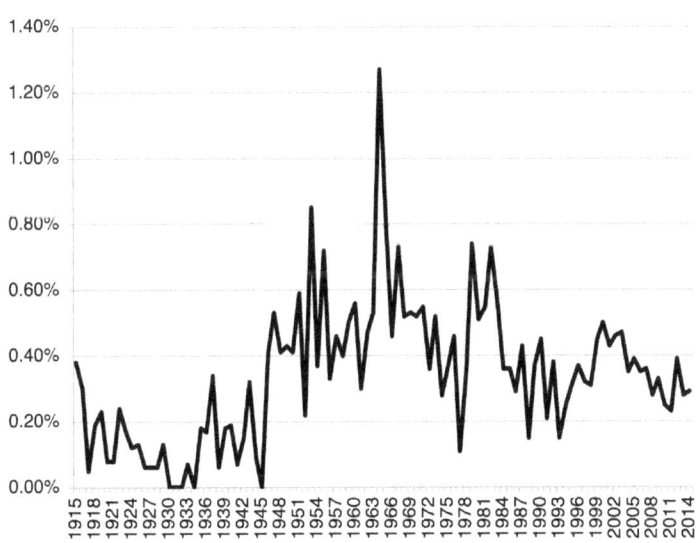

Figure 3.2 Shakespeare on screen, 1915–2014, showing relative popularity.

Despite its popularity, Shakespeare on TV is often judged negatively. Usually it just doesn't work.[4] Sometimes it's as simple as low production values and bad acting, but there's also a deeper problem. Something about the serial form of television—where programs repeat nightly or weekly (not to mention yearly) in half- or full-hour chunks— is a bad fit for the "two-hours' traffic" of Shakespeare's plays (*Romeo and Juliet*, Pr.12). Those plays seem better suited for film. The one clear case of successful television Shakespeare is the history plays, which, like television shows, work according to episodes strung together to tell a long, sprawling narrative that just keeps going and going. As series such as Peter Dews's *An Age of Kings* (1960), John Barton and Peter Hall's *The Wars of the Roses* (1965), the BBC Television Shakespeare (1978–85), and *The Hollow Crown* (2012–16) illustrate, television can work for the history plays.

In the 1970s, academic Shakespeare studies started catching up to the general public's fascination with new modern art connected in some way to Shakespeare. The earliest and most enduring question has been about finding the right terms to capture the varieties. Moving from least to most radical, we see the *abridgments* and *emendations* commonly done in straightforward performances (a line or a scene is cut for the sake of time). We see *alterations, ameliorations, distortions, modifications, mutilations,* and *revisions* (as in the censorship of Shakespeare's sexual material during the Franco Regime in Spain). We see *translations* of the text into different languages (such as the UK government donating £1.5m to translate the complete works of Shakespeare into Mandarin). We see *additions* and *interpolations* (as in the seven new passages Colly Cibber added to his *Richard III* [1699]). We see pastiches that mash up multiple scenes from different plays (such as William Davenant's *The Law against Lovers* [1662], combining *Measure for Measure* and *Much Ado about Nothing*). We see *burlesques, travesties,* and *satires* that send up the Shakespearean original in absurdist terms (these were popular in the nineteenth century and have recently re-emerged in examples such as the Reduced Shakespeare Company's *The Complete Works of William Shakespeare (Abridged)* [1987]). We see *adaptations, conversions,* and *metamorphoses* that shift the text into a different medium (such as Charles and Mary Lamb's *Tales from Shakespeare* [1807], Giuseppe Verdi's *Falstaff* [1893], the Royal Shakespeare Company's *Such Tweet Sorrow* [2010, a Twitter version of *Romeo and Juliet*], or Punchdrunk's *Sleep No More* [2011, an immersive theater version of *Macbeth*]). We see *allusions* and *citations* (as when the Broadway musical *Hamilton* [2016] draws an analogy between the American Revolution and *Macbeth*). We see *amplifications, augmentations, collaborations,* and *fan fictions* that narrate what Shakespeare left out, often a character's pre-Shakespearean past or post-Shakespearean future (the very first was John Fletcher's *The Woman's Prize: Or, the Tamer Tamed* [1611]; others include Robert Browning's "Caliban upon Setebos" [1864] and John Updike's *Gertrude and Claudius* [2009]). We see *reconfigurations, re-visions, re-envisionings, re-makes, re-workings, re-tellings,* and *re-writings* that narrate the same story as Shakespeare, but not in the same way (as in Tom Stoppard's *Rosencrantz and Guildenstern are Dead* [1966], an existentialist riff on *Hamlet*; Aimé Césaire's *Une Tempête* [1969], *The Tempest* from the colonized perspective; or Preti Taneja's *We That are Young* [2018], which re-sets *King Lear* in present-day India). We see *appropriations* that use Shakespeare, his texts, and his cultural capital for their own purposes, sometimes making this indebtedness clear (as in Cole Porter's *Kiss Me, Kate* [1948, based on *Taming of the Shrew*] or Barbara Garson's *Macbird!* [1966, based on *Macbeth*]), sometimes not (as with *Strange Brew* [1983, based on *Hamlet*] or *My Own Private Idaho* [1991, based on *1 Henry IV*]. We see *imitations,* texts written in the manner of Shakespeare, whether seriously (as in John Keats's *King Stephen* [1819]) or humorously (as in Ian Doescher's *William Shakespeare's Star Wars* [2013]). And we see general *intertextualities* which mingle bits from Shakespeare's life and works into their original narratives (such as *Shakespeare Wallah* [1965], about a Shakespearean acting trope in India; *Theater of Blood* [1973], about a Shakespearean actor taking revenge on his critics; or *Shakespeare in Love* [1998], which re-imagines Shakespeare writing *Romeo and Juliet*).

In the earliest book on the subject, Ruby Cohn opted for the umbrella term *Modern Shakespearean Offshoots* (1976), emphasizing "how far the shoots grow from the Shakespearean stem."[5] Fifteen years later, Jean Marsden edited *The Appropriation of Shakespeare*, drawing attention to the negative connotations of this term: "Associated with abduction, adoption and theft, appropriation's central tenet is the desire for possession.... Appropriation is neither dispassionate nor disinterested; it has connotations of usurpation, of seizure for one's own uses."[6] Years later, Marsden defined *adaptation* as "significant changes made to a pre-existing literary work," noting that "a play which has Shakespeare as its source but which itself represents a totally different work" is not an adaptation; it's something else (notionally an *appropriation*).[7] But not everyone agrees on these definitions, as discussed in the anthologies of Shakespearean off-shoots that started appearing in the late 1990s (using the term *adaptations* in their titles, but presenting mostly what earlier scholars called *appropriations*).[8]

The negative connotations of the term *appropriation* didn't fit all texts working off Shakespeare to create new art, as Christy Desmet and Robert Sawyer argued in 1999, developing earlier arguments about commercial exploitation: "'Big-time Shakespeare' serves corporate goals, entrenched power structures, and conservative cultural ideologies. 'Small-time Shakespeare,' which emerges from local, more pointed responses to the Bard, satisfies motives ranging from play, to political commitment, to agonistic gamesmanship."[9] Another issue was that, as Margaret Kidnie observed in 2009, "Adaptation keeps emerging as a 'problem' for production since the work itself adapts over time."[10] Adaptation is already at work in what we like to think of as straightforward performance. That's partly why in 2015 Christy Desmet and Sujata Iyengar argued "the difference between adaptation and appropriation, from a theoretical and historical perspective, proves to be a difference in degree rather than kind."[11] And that argument helps to explain why, in the journal they founded in 2005, Desmet and Iyengar opted for the title *Borrowers and Lenders: A Journal of Shakespeare and Appropriation.*[12]

These terminological quibbles have only been exacerbated by Shakespeare's migration into "a plethora of contemporary formats—novel, horror, screenplay, musical—in foreign performance traditions—*kathakali, theerukootu,* and *kudiattam,* for example—and in a bewildering range of media forms, from film via video to DVD, CD-ROM, and the internet."[13] Shakespeare scholars must now reckon with "the increasingly heterogeneous and fragmentary presence of 'Shakespeare' in the increasingly digitized and globalized mediascape of the beginning of the twenty-first century."[14] Amidst the rise of new digital media forms, "intermediality has played and will continue to play a significant role in testing what we mean by Shakespearean adaptation."[15]

With the expanding reach of recent Shakespearean offshoots, a new line of thought has emerged: the Not-Shakespeare discourse. This field attends to the blurry and shifting line between adaptation (that is still recognizably Shakespearean) and appropriation (that may not be). For, as Marjorie Garber observed in 2009, "The word 'Shakespearean' today has taken on its own set of connotations, often quite distinct from any reference to Shakespeare or his plays."[16] To be "Shakespearean," she points out, is sometimes simply to be big, serious, complex, and/or tragic, even with no direct connection to Shakespeare at all. Arguably, that is the sense in which *Game of Thrones* is a "Shakespearean" text. As Graham Holderness wrote in 2014, "That which is not Shakespeare has an uncanny way of becoming Shakespeare, and *vice versa.*"[17] This notion formed the basis of a 2017 collection of essays titled *Shakespeare / Not Shakespeare*:

> Something—a play, a film, an object, a story—may not merely resemble its corollary in the Shakespearean canon, but perhaps more puzzling, at once "be" and "not be" Shakespeare. This phenomenon can be a matter of perception rather than authorial intention (audiences may detect Shakespeare where the author disclaims him or may have difficulty finding him where he is named); it may equally be a product of intertextual and intermedial relations, processes that work on the level of semiotics and material substrate, apart from more overt processes of influence and reception.[18]

In Peter Kirwin's words, "Not-Shakespeare is and is not a form of Shakespearean performance."[19]

The most sustained theme in the Not-Shakespeare discourse is the effort to find the right metaphor to describe the situation. In a 2005 essay, Holderness tried out *beeswax* (which seems both solid and mutable), *metallurgy* (malleability, plasticity, ductility), *protein* ("the building blocks of life"), *subterranean fungus* (only connected deep below the surface), a *black hole* (pulling everything toward it with a huge gravitational force), and *the big bang* (that singular moment out of which the universe grew).[20] In 2014, he tried out the metaphor of *collision*, where two objects crash into each other, releasing new energy: "the 'Shakespeare' generated from such collisions does not necessarily resemble what [we] think of as 'Shakespeare' at all" (17). Also in 2014, Douglas Lanier (drawing upon Deleuze and Guattari) used the metaphor of *rhizomes*, plants like ground cover that spread horizontally by shooting off buds beneath the soil, in contrast to trees, which have a clearly connected root structure all moving toward a strong center, which then produces the branches that grow from it:

> Shakespearean rhizomatics includes Shakespeare the text but is in no way reducible to it; it also necessarily includes faithful and unfaithful adaptations, and adaptations of them, and adaptations of *them*. And by its nature the Shakespearean rhizome is never a stable object but an aggregated field in a perpetual state of becoming, ever being reconfigured as new adaptations intersect with and grow from it.[21]

In 2015, Kevin Wetmore and Adam Hansen opted for the metaphor of the *echo*, that faint, disembodied repetition bouncing off canyon walls.[22] They also used the *ghost*: "Shakespeare haunts many texts," they wrote, noting that "subtle Shakespearean presence can be difficult to detect" (17). And in 2017, Kristin Denslow turned to the *meme*, "a term associated with Internet culture but coined by Richard Dawkins to describe a unit of cultural transmission," to describe "how versions of Shakespeare's texts, narratives, and themes replicate and proliferate in popular culture, in important respects decoupled from the text of the play and its standing in the artistic and critical canon."[23]

The most compelling metaphor is probably the most obvious: the *world*, what some scholars call the *Shakesphere*, understood as an entire universe or microcosm in which Shakespearean creation and activity occurs. In 2000, Bryan Reynolds and Donald Hedrick called it *Shakespace*, "the territory within discourses, adaptations, and uses of Shakespeare."[24] In 2014, Daniel Fischlin drew attention "from traditional Shakespeare-centric interpretation to the 'outerspeares,' the 'outer spheres,' the marginal or exploratory sites where non-traditional interpretations of non-traditional forms of the Shakespeare effect are in evidence."[25] Within this vast space, the uses of Shakespeare are infinite, leading Valerie Fazel and Louise Geddes to theorize "the Shakespeare user" as anyone who engages with Shakespeare in any way whatsoever, whether it's reading, studying, performing, adapting, appropriating, exploiting, or what have you.[26]

Because it evinces so many of these features of modern Shakespearean manifestation—including its contested status as officially Shakespearean—*Game of Thrones* is the über-offshoot of Shakespeare, one which clearly draws from the "Shakesphere" but also hovers elusively in the "Outerspeares"; one which is "Shakespearean" but also "Not-Shakespeare"; one where Shakespeare is felt as an echo, a haunting, or a meme; and one which illustrates the Shakespearean slingshot.

In a general sense, the Shakespearean slingshot is a common technique. Artists position themselves behind Shakespeare, drafting off his cultural energy, allowing his power and popularity to clear the way for new artistic endeavors, the artists darting out from behind Shakespeare at key moments, taking the lead, going in their own directions, leaving him behind to fade into the distance. But in the specific sense I want to develop, the Shakespearean slingshot is closely related to Peak TV. *Sons of Anarchy*, *House of Cards*, *Empire*, *Star-Crossed*, and *Vice Principals* are the clearest examples of Shakespearean adaptations that then drift away from the initial conceit, a phenomenon closely associated with their form as multi-year television shows, as opposed to films.

Sons of Anarchy started out as *Hamlet*, with Jax Teller as Prince Hamlet, John Teller as King Hamlet, Clay Marrow as Claudius, and

Gemma Teller-Marrow as Gertrude.²⁷ After that initial set-up, the show drifted from the plot of *Hamlet*, not only to focus on the contemporary culture of motorcycle clubs, but also when character parallels broke down. Most notably, Ophelia was split between Tara Knowles, the protagonist's love interest, and the character whose name actually recalls Ophelia, Opie Winston, whose father dies, leading to madness and eventually death.

House of Cards started as *Richard III*, with Frank Underwood as Richard, President Walker as Edward IV, and Doug Stamper as the Duke of Buckingham.²⁸ The show followed the play pretty closely until the end of Season 2, when Frank becomes president, corresponding to Act IV, Scene ii in *Richard III*. The show then veered away from the play, in large part because *House of Cards* kept getting renewed for more and more seasons. It had more stories to tell in the relatively short space left in Shakespeare's play between Richard's ascension to the throne and his defeat at the Battle of Bosworth.

Empire started as *King Lear*, with Lucious as Lear, the ailing patriarch who must decide which child will inherit his empire.²⁹ But the plot of the show strayed in several ways. It drew equally from *The Lion in Winter*. It became more organically oriented to modern hip hop and corporate culture. And it brought in a number of non-*Lear* references to Shakespeare, with Rhonda emerging as a Lady Macbeth figure, and episode titles like "The Devil Quotes Scripture" (*Merchant of Venice*, 1.3.91), "Unto the Breach" (*Henry V*, 3.1.1), and "Out, Damned Spot!" (*Macbeth*, 5.1.30).

The 2009 ABC Family series *10 Things I Hate about You* was a television adaptation of the film appropriation of Shakespeare's *Taming of the Shrew*. Like the film, the series then strayed from Shakespeare's plot to focus on the troubles of American teens. Following a similar trajectory, the CW series *Star-Crossed* started as *Romeo and Juliet*, aliens as Montagues and humans as Capulets, Roman a Romeo, and Emery a Juliet.³⁰ But then the series strayed from Shakespeare's plot to delve into topics ranging from high school life to race relations and the media. This swerve is best illustrated by the episode titles all being quotations from *Romeo and Juliet*, but not in the order that they occur in Shakespeare's play.

Finally, the HBO series *Vice Principals* started out as *Othello* for American high school teachers, with Principle Belinda Brown as Othello and vice principals Neal Gamby and Lee Russell combining to form Iago.³¹ The first season followed the plot of *Othello* in broad strokes, Gamby and Russell conspiring to destroy Brown, whose name indicates the racial overtones of the show. But that left Season 2 with a question: What do you do with a show based on Shakespeare that outlives the five acts already plotted? *Vice Principals* turned into a comic who-dun-it that wasn't Shakespearean at all.

Not all recent Shakespearean television exhibits the Shakespearean slingshot. There are occasional Shakespeare allusions and quotations in *Lost*.[32] And, to a greater extent, Shakespeare is quoted in *Westworld*.[33] But the plots of those shows are not derived from Shakespeare's. There are vaguely Shakespearean themes and characters in *Breaking Bad*, which have drawn comparisons to plays like *Macbeth*.[34] But those are instances of broad analogy rather than direct influence. And there were witty riffs on Shakespeare's life in the BBC series *Upstart Crow* and the TNT series *Will*. But those are not Shakespearean slingshots in the sense that they pattern their initial conceits upon one of his plays and then move away from it to address other concerns.

Similarly, *Game of Thrones* is not a perfect Shakespearean slingshot. It is not simply an unacknowledged or unadvertised adaptation of a Shakespearean text. It is arguably an unconscious adaptation of a Shakespearean discourse. It does not slingshot off Shakespeare as much as it slingshots off the Shakesphere, the broad discourse of Shakespearean usage which is already one step removed from the original texts. *Game of Thrones* is a Shakespherean slingshot (note the spelling). The work's literary indebtedness to Shakespeare is complex and difficult to decipher because, in contrast to the direct Shakespearean slingshot, the Shakespherean slingshot exhibits at least two clearly defined layers of separation from any Shakespearean "source."

What is also fascinating about *Game of Thrones* is that there was a reverse Shakespearean slingshot off it, in keeping with Lanier's observation of a mutually exploitative relationship between Shakespeare and pop culture. As Marina Gerzic discusses, *The Hollow Crown*, especially the second series, was repeatedly reviewed as "Shakespeare outdoes *Game of Thrones*."[35] In the words of David Hinckley, "Pound for pound, the drama in *The Hollow Crown* matches almost everything in *Game of Thrones*."[36] One of the lead actors in *The Hollow Crown*, Hugh Bonneville, penned a passionate celebration of Shakespeare by drafting off the cultural energy of *Game of Thrones*.[37] Similarly, Justin Kurzel and Michael Fassbender's *Macbeth* was plugged as "Shakespeare meets *Game of Thrones*."[38] And reviews and promotional materials for a number of recent Shakespearean theatrical productions have billed them as "Shakespeare for the *Game of Thrones* generation."[39] In these cases, the Shakespeare who led the way for so long but then faded into the background—the writer who carved a cultural space for tragedy in mainstream art, allowing later writers to draft behind his lead, until they shoot out from behind him to pursue their own artistic concerns quite distinct from his—was found drafting off a modern text already indebted to him, *Game of Thrones*, using its cultural momentum to slingshot out from behind it.

Notes

1. See Megan Garber, David Sims, Lenika Cruz, and Sophie Gilbert, "Have We Reached 'Peak TV'?" *The Atlantic* (Aug. 12, 2015), https://www.theatlantic.com/entertainment/archive/2015/08/have-we-reached-peak-tv/401009/.
2. See Terence Hawkes, "Bardbiz," *The London Review of Books* (Feb. 20, 1990): 11–13; Michael D. Bristol, *Big-Time Shakespeare* (New York: Routledge, 1996).
3. Douglas Lanier, "Recent Shakespeare Adaptation and the Mutations of Cultural Capital," *Shakespeare Studies* 38 (2010): 104.
4. See, for example, the negative judgments of Olwen Terris, "Shakespeare and British Television," *Shakespeare Survey* 61 (2008): 199–212.
5. Ruby Cohn, *Modern Shakespeare Offshoots* (Princeton: Princeton University Press, 1976), 3.
6. *The Appropriation of Shakespeare: Post-Renaissance Reconstructions of the Works and the Myth*, ed. Jean Marsden (New York: Hemel Hempstead, 1991), 1.
7. Jean I. Marsden, *The Re-imagined Text: Shakespeare, Adaptation, and Eighteenth-Century Literary Theory* (Lexington: University Press of Kentucky, 1995), 7–8.
8. See *Shakespeare Made Fit: Restoration Adaptations of Shakespeare*, ed. Sandra Clark (London: J.M. Dent, 1997); *Adaptations of Shakespeare*, ed. Daniel Fischlin and Mark Fortier Fischlin (New York: Routledge, 2000).
9. *Shakespeare and Appropriation*, ed. Christy Desmet and Robert O. Sawyer (New York: Routledge, 1999), 2.
10. Margaret Jane Kidnie, *Shakespeare and the Problem of Adaptation* (New York: Routledge, 2009), 9.
11. Christy Desmet and Sujata Iyengar, "Adaptation, Appropriation, or What you Will," *Shakespeare* 11.1 (2015), 16.
12. *Borrowers and Lenders: A Journal of Shakespeare and Appropriation*, ed. Christy Desmet and Sujata Iyengar (2005-Press), http://www.borrowers.uga.edu.
13. *Remaking Shakespeare*, ed. Pascale Aebischer, Edward J. Esche, and Nigel Wheale (London: Palgrave Macmillan, 2003), 4.
14. Maurizio Calbi, *Spectral Shakespeares: Media Adaptations in the Twenty-First Century* (New York: Palgrave Macmillan, 2013), 2.
15. Daniel Fischlin, Introduction to *OuterSpeares: Shakespeare, Intermedia, and the Limits of Adaptation*, ed. Daniel Fischlin (Toronto: University of Toronto Press, 2014), 35.
16. Marjorie Garber, *Shakespeare and Modern Culture* (Cambridge: Harvard University Press, 2009), xiv.
17. Graham Holderness, *Tales from Shakespeare: Creative Collisions* (Cambridge: Cambridge University Press, 2014), 225.

34 *The Shakespearean slingshot*

18 *Shakespeare/Not Shakespeare*, ed. Christy Desmet, Natalie Loper, and Jim Casey (New York: Palgrave Macmillan, 2017).
19 Peter Kirwin, "Not-Shakespeare and the Shakespearean Ghost," in *The Oxford Handbook of Shakespeare and Performance*, ed. James C. Bulman (Oxford: Oxford University Press, 2017), 88. Kirwin was writing here about modern performances of non-Shakespearean Renaissance dramatists, but we can adapt—appropriate—his point for those appropriations where one feels a Shakespearean presence that is never advertised or acknowledged.
20 Graham Holderness, "'Dressing Old Words New': Shakespeare, Science, and Appropriation," *Borrowers and Lenders* 1.2 (2005), https://borrowers.uga.edu/781442/show.
21 Douglas Lanier, "Shakespearean Rhizomatics: Adaptation, Ethics, Value," in *Shakespeare and the Ethics of Appropriation*, ed. Alexander Huang and Elizabeth Rivlin (New York: Palgrave, 2014), 29–30.
22 *Shakespearean Echoes*, ed. Kevin J. Wetmore and Adam Hansen, Jr., (New York: Palgrave Macmillan, 2015), 17.
23 Kristin N. Denslow, "Guest Starring *Hamlet*: The Proliferation of the Shakespeare Meme on American Television," in *Shakespeare / Not Shakespeare*, ed. Christy Desmet, Natalie Loper, and Jim Casey (New York: Palgrave Macmillan, 2017), 97.
24 Bryan Reynolds and Donald Hedrick, "Shakespace and Transversal Power," in *Shakespeare without Class: Misappropriations of Cultural Capital*, ed. Reynolds and Hendrick (New York: Palgrave, 2000), 1. See also Bryan Reynolds, *Transversal Subjects: From Montaigne to Deleuze after Derrida* (New York: Palgrave Macmillan, 2009), which gives a glossary definition of "Shakespace":

> An example of articulatory space, particularly potent both in scholarly currencies due to Shakespeare's prominence in major cross-disciplinary discourses and in various popular cultures insofar as Shakespeare dominates theatrical production worldwide. Touching upon seemingly every facet of critical practices, Shakespace comprises a nexus of transversal power, capable of generating and intensifying transversal movements through the constant renegotiation of its imbricated discourses and phenomena. Additionally, the term Shakespeare acts metonymically as a method to understanding articulatory spaces as a whole, and thus can serve pedagogically as an entryway into transversal poetics.
>
> (283)

25 Daniel Fischlin, Introduction to *OuterSpeares: Shakespeare, Intermedia, and the Limits of Adaptation*, ed. Daniel Fischlin (Toronto: University of Toronto Press, 2014), 4.
26 Valerie M. Fazel and Louise Geddes, "The Shakespeare User," in *The Shakespeare User: Critical and Creative Appropriations in a Networked Culture*, ed. Valerie M. Fazel and Louise Gedded (New York: Palgrave Macmillan, 2017), 1–22.
27 See Sylvaine Bataille, "'*Hamlet* on Harleys': Sons of Anarchy's Appropriation of *Hamlet*," in *Shakespeare on Screen: Hamlet*, ed. Sarah Hatchuel and Nathalie Vienne-Guerrin (Mont-Saint-Aignan: Publications des

Universités de Rouen et du Havre, 2011), 329–44; Noel Sloboda, "Hamlet In (and Off) Stages: Television, Serialization, and Shakespeare in *Sons of Anarchy*," *Journal of the Wooden O Symposium* 12 (2012): 85–99; Jessica Walker, "Incapable of His Own Distress: Genderbending Ophelia," in *Bonds of Brotherhood in Sons of Anarchy: Essays on Masculinity in the FX Series*, ed. Susan Fanetti (Jefferson: McFarland & Co., 2018): 65–76.
28 See Jeffrey R. Wilson, "Villainy and Complicity in Drama, Television, and Politics: Shakespeare's *Richard III*, *House of Cards*, and the Trump Administration," in *Shakespeare and Trump* (Philadelphia: Temple University Press, 2020), 99–128.
29 See Folger Shakespeare Library, "How 'King Lear' Inspired 'Empire'," *Shakespeare Unlimited* (March 22, 2017), https://www.folger.edu/shakespeare-unlimited/empire-ilene-chaiken.
30 See Kinga Földváry, "Serial Shakespeare: The Case of Star-Crossed (2014)," *Between: Rivista dell'Associazione di Teoria e Storia Comparata della Letteratura* 6.11 (2016): 1–22, http://ojs.unica.it/index.php/between/article/view/2073.
31 See James Newlin, "Foul Pranks: Recognizing *Vice Principals* as a Comic *Othello*," *Shakespeare Bulletin* 36.2 (2018): 197–223.
32 See Kathryn Stockton, "Lost, or 'Exit, Pursued by a Bear': Causing Queer Children on Shakespeare's TV," in *Shakesqueer: A Queer Companion to the Complete Works of Shakespeare*, ed. Madhavi Menon (Durham: Duke University Press, 2011), 421–28; Sarah Hatchuel and Randy Laist, "Lost: Une «Romance» Shakespearienne?" *TV/Series Hors Séries* 1 (2016): http://tvseries.revues.org/1656; Sarah Hatchuel and Anaïs Pauchet, "Shakespeare en Séries: Des Intrigues, des Mots et des Spectres," *Positif* 670 (2016): 106–8; Todd Landon Barnes, "The *Tempest*'s 'Standing Water': Echoes of Early Modern Cosmographies in *Lost*," in *Shakespearean Echoes*, ed. Kevin J. Wetmore and Adam Hansen, Jr. (New York: Palgrave Macmillan, 2015), 168–85.
33 See Reto Winckler, "This Great Stage of Androids: *Westworld*, Shakespeare, and the World as Stage," *Journal of Adaptation in Film & Performance* 10.2 (2017): 169–88.
34 See Tom Gualtieri, "Walter White vs. Macbeth," *Salon* (Aug. 10, 2013), https://www.salon.com/2013/08/10/walter_white_vs_macbeth/.
35 See Marina Gerzic, "Re-fashioning Richard III: Intertextuality, Fandom, and the (Mobile) Body in *The Hollow Crown: The Wars of the Roses*," in *From Medievalism to Early-Modernism: Adapting the English Past*, ed. Marina Gerzic and Aidan Norrie (New York: Routledge, 2019), 192–95; Michael Billington, "Shakespeare Outdoes *Game of Thrones* in the BBC's *Hollow Crown*," *The Guardian* (May 7, 2016), https://www.theguardian.com/stage/theatreblog/2016/may/07/shakespeare-game-of-thrones-bbc-hollow-crown.
36 David Hinckley, "*The Hollow Crown*: TV Review," *NY Daily News* (Sept. 20, 2013), http://www.nydailynews.com/entertainment/hollow-crown-tv-review-article-1.1461321.
37 Hugh Bonneville, "Shakespeare Gives Us as Much Lust and Violence as Any Episode of *Game of Thrones*," *Radio Times* (Oct. 13, 2014), http://www.radiotimes.com/news/2014-10-13/hugh-bonneville-shakespeare-gives-us-as-much-lust-and-violence-as-any-episode-of-game-ofthrones.

38 See Graham Flanagan, "The New 'Macbeth' Movie Looks Like Shakespeare Meets 'Game of Thrones'," *Business Insider* (June 6, 2015), https://www.businessinsider.com/macbeth-movie-trailer-2015-6.
39 See Ben Brantley, "Review: Shakespeare's Take on the *Game of Thrones*," *New York Times* (Nov. 4, 2016), https://www.nytimes.com/2016/11/05/theater/review-shakespeares-take-on-the-game-of-thrones.html; Amanda McLoone, "Shakespeare for the Game of Thrones generation," *Millennium Forum Theatre & Conference Centre* (Jan. 9, 2017), https://www.millenniumforum.co.uk/shakespeare-game-thrones-generation/.

4 Composition history and co(rporate)-authorship

In 2016, *The New Oxford Shakespeare* made international headlines, announcing that computer-aided scholarship suggested that 12 of Shakespeare's plays were written in collaboration with other authors.[1] Shakespeare also "collaborated" with the authors of his sources, and with Elizabethan theater-makers.[2] Many hands went into Shakespeare's stories, especially the histories at the start of his career—presenting parallels between early-modern playwrighting and corporate Hollywood authorship that films like *Shakespeare in Love* (1998) have explored.[3]

According to the *New Oxford* chronology, Shakespeare, Christopher Marlowe, and others wrote the play we now call *2 Henry VI* first, probably around 1590. *2 Henry VI* was performed in 1590–91, maybe by Lord Strange's Men or Lord Pembroke's Men. Then, probably around 1591, Shakespeare, Marlowe, and others wrote the play we now call *3 Henry VI* as a "sequel" to the earlier *2 Henry VI*. About a year later, as another sequel to those two *Henry VI* plays, Shakespeare wrote *Richard III* by himself, making a "trilogy" of plays. Probably in early 1592, the play we now call *1 Henry VI* was written by Thomas Nashe, Marlowe, maybe Shakespeare (or maybe his contributions were written later), and probably others. If this timeline is correct, then *1 Henry VI* was written as a "prequel" to *2* and *3 Henry VI*, making a "tetralogy" of plays (*1, 2,* and *3 Henry VI* plus *Richard III*). Later in 1592, *1 Henry VI* was performed by Lord Strange's Men. It was a huge success. Then, early in 1592, one or both of *2* and *3 Henry VI* were performed by Pembroke's Men. That same year, *Richard III* was performed by Pembroke's Men. It was Shakespeare's first big hit. In 1594, *The First Part of the Contention* (i.e., *2 Henry VI*) was first published in a shorter, alternate form from what was later published in the first folio (there would be three editions before 1640). In 1594–95, all three of the *Henry VI* plays were performed by the newly formed Lord Chamberlain's Men, where Shakespeare was a founding member. It may be at this point that Shakespeare added his scenes to *1 Henry VI* and revised sections of *2* and *3 Henry VI*. In 1595, *The Tragedy of Richard, Duke of York, and Death of Good King Henry the Sixth* (i.e., *3 Henry VI*) was first published (there would be three editions before 1640).

"From then onwards," Stanley Wells writes, "perhaps with a sigh of relief, he became his own master"—Shakespeare collaborated with co-authors less frequently.[4] Around 1595, he wrote *Richard II*, a solely authored work, starting the sequence of four history plays known as his "second tetralogy," which served as a prequel to his "first tetralogy." Shakespeare then wrote *1 Henry IV* in 1597, *2 Henry IV* in 1598, and *Henry V* in 1599, completing his second tetralogy before going on to write his famous tragedies such as *Hamlet, Othello, King Lear,* and *Macbeth*.

The compositional history of *Game of Thrones* is even more complicated. The idea for *A Song of Ice and Fire* first came to Martin in 1991, but it wasn't until 1994 that he acquired a contract for a trilogy of novels to include *A Game of Thrones, A Dance with Dragons,* and *The Winds of Winter*.[5] Even before finishing *A Game of Thrones*, Martin knew he needed more than a trilogy. *A Game of Thrones* was published in 1996; the sequel, *A Clash of Kings*, in 1998; the third book, *A Storm of Swords*, in 2000; and the fourth, *A Feast for Crows*, in 2005. Also in 2005, writers David Benioff and D.B. Weiss met with Martin to discuss a television adaptation. In 2006, Benioff and Weiss pitched the show to HBO, which eventually acquired the rights to *A Song of Ice and Fire* in 2008.[6] At this point, to quote Jerome Christensen, "the studio, not the director, screenwriter, or even producer should be regarded as the author."[7]

After pre-production and casting, a pilot episode was filmed in late 2009. The show was picked up by HBO in early 2010. And the first season was shot by the end of the year. After a vigorous promotional campaign, the show premiered under the title *Game of Thrones* on HBO to 4.2 million viewers on April 17, 2011.[8] Here the authorship of *Game of Thrones* was further complicated as the brand expanded from novel series and television show to exhibit what Zoë Shacklock calls a "transmedia textuality," including (on the one hand) promotional materials, games, cook books, toys, and other paratexts authored by HBO, and (on the other) conventions, cultural commentary, fan art, and fan fiction authored by audiences.[9]

Based on the show's success, HBO renewed it for a second season, which filmed in 2011. Also fast on the heels of the show's success at

HBO, Martin published the fifth book in the novel series, *A Dance with Dragons*, in 2011. At that time, Martin had already finished several chapters of his planned sixth book, titled *The Winds of Winter*, but this book was delayed due to an influx of Martin's speaking engagements and other projects. Meanwhile, the show churned along, releasing a new season each year, raising the possibility that the story being told in the show might surpass the books. Martin was not worried in 2013: "Long before they catch up with me, I'll have published *The Winds of Winter*, which'll give me another couple years. It might be tight on the last book, *A Dream of Spring*, as they juggernaut forward."[10] With the show in its fourth season in 2014, Martin published *The World of Ice & Fire: The Untold History of Westeros and the Game of Thrones*. With *The Winds of Winter* still incomplete, the author was less optimistic in 2016: "The show has caught up and is in the process of passing me."[11] Airing in 2016, Season 6 of the show was the first to move beyond the books, the HBO writers aware of how Martin was planning to end his narrative, but now themselves the primary authors responsible for writing the show's conclusion. It seems that Martin discovered, to quote Michael Szalay's reading of the title sequence of *Game of Thrones*, that "story emerges from brand equity as earth and rock emerge from magma, or as coins emerge from molten gold."[12]

In 2018, Martin published *Fire & Blood*, a novel culled from material cut from *The World of Ice & Fire*. The HBO series aired its eighth and final season in 2019. *The Winds of Winter* has not been published as of this writing. *A Dream of Spring* is a dream indeed. A second volume of *Fire & Blood* is expected. Meanwhile, HBO has pushed ahead, hearing pitches for five possible spin-offs, greenlighting one, a prequel series set thousands of years before *Game of Thrones*, titled *The Long Night*, which was scheduled to begin shooting in 2019, but then cancelled in October 2019. A different spin-off, called *House of the Dragon*, based on *Fire & Blood*, was announced in January 2020. There may be as many as three additional series on the way.[13]

Thus, where the Elizabethan theatrical scene of Shakespeare's London boasted a system of collaborative authorship that identified young talent and fostered the careers of individual artists—allowing for the emergence of the man who would become the most celebrated author in the English language—the twenty-first-century American entertainment industry exhibits a system of corporate authorship that literally takes authors' narratives away from them for the sake of making money.

Notes

1. See *The New Oxford Shakespeare: Authorship Companion*, ed. Gary Taylor and Gabriel Egan (Oxford: Oxford University Press, 2017), esp. the summative Chapter 25, Gary Taylor and Rory Loughnane's "The Canon and Chronology of Shakespeare's Works" (417–602).
2. See Ton Hoenselaars, "Shakespeare: Colleagues, Collaborators, Co-authors," in *The Cambridge Companion to Shakespeare and Contemporary Dramatists*, ed. Ton Hoenselaars (Cambridge: Cambridge University Press, 2012), 97–119.
3. See Martin Harries, "Hollywood in Love," *The Chronicle Review* (April 16, 1999), https://www.chronicle.com/article/Hollywood-in-Love/24336.
4. Stanley Wells, *Shakespeare and Co.: Christopher Marlowe, Thomas Dekker, Ben Jonson, Thomas Middleton, John Fletcher and the Other Players in His Story* (London: Allen Lane, 2006), 208.
5. See Dave Itzkoff, "His Beautiful Dark Twisted Fantasy: George R. R. Martin Talks 'Game of Thrones'," *New York Times* (April 1, 2011), https://artsbeat.blogs.nytimes.com/2011/04/01/his-beautiful-dark-twisted-fantasy-george-r-r-martin-talks-game-of-thrones/.
6. See "Production Timeline," *Game of Thrones Wiki*, http://gameofthrones.wikia.com/wiki/Production_timeline.
7. Jerome Christensen, *America's Corporate Art: The Studio Authorship of Hollywood Motion Pictures* (Palo Alto: Stanford University Press, 2012), vii. On HBO as a corporate author, see *It's Not TV: Watching HBO in the Post-Television Era*, ed. Marc Leverette, Brian L. Ott, and Cara Louise Buckley (New York: Routledge, 2008).
8. See James Hibbard, "'Game of Thrones' Premiere Ratings are In," *Entertainment Weekly* (April 19, 2011), http://www.ew.com/article/2011/04/19/game-of-thrones-premiere-ratings/.
9. See Zoë Shacklock, "'A Reader Lives a Thousand Lives before He Dies': Transmedia Textuality and the Flows of Adaptation," in *Mastering the Game of Thrones: Essays on George R.R. Martin's A Song of Ice and Fire*, ed. Jes Battis and Susan Johnston (Jefferson: McFarland, 2015), 262–80. See also Andrew Howe, "The Hand of the Artist: Fan Art in the Martinverse," in *Mastering the Game of Thrones*, 243–61; Katharine Sarikakis, Claudia Krug, and Joan Ramon Rodriguez-Amat, "Defining Authorship in User-Generated Content: Copyright Struggles in *The Game of Thrones*," *New Media & Society* 19.4 (2017): 542–59; and *Fan Phenomena: Game of Thrones*, ed. Kavita Mudan Finn (Bristol: Intellect, 2017).
10. "George R.R. Martin Has a Detailed Plan for Keeping the Game of Thrones TV Show from Catching Up To Him," *Vanity Fair* (March 11, 2014), https://www.vanityfair.com/hollywood/2014/03/george-r-r-martin-interview.
11. Terri Schwartz, "Game of Thrones Will Never Be Able to Do This Winds of Winter Twist," *IGN* (Feb. 25, 2016), http://www.ign.com/articles/2016/02/25/game-of-thrones-will-never-be-able-to-do-this-winds-of-winter-twist?watch.
12. Michael Szalay, "HBO's Flexible Gold," *Representations* 126.1 (2014): 113.
13. Aja Romano, "HBO's Game of Thrones Prequels: What We Know So Far," *Vox* (updated Jan. 16, 2020), https://www.vox.com/2019/11/4/20940933/game-of-thrones-prequels-spinoffs-hbo-updates-what-we-know.

5 From true tragedy to historical fantasy

Why was Martin drawn to the Wars of the Roses for source material when writing his fantasy novels? He wasn't. *Game of Thrones* began with English history: "The Wall predates anything else," Martin says. "I can trace back the inspiration for that to 1981. I was in England visiting a friend, and as we approached the border of England and Scotland, we stopped to see Hadrian's Wall."[1] Then came the Wars of the Roses: "I did consider at a very early stage—going all the way back to 1991—whether to include overt fantasy elements, and at one point thought of writing a Wars of the Roses novel."[2] Martin did not start with fantasy, then add history. He started with the Wars of the Roses, then realized that that story he sought to tell had affinities to the genre of fantasy. So how did Martin get from medieval English kings and queens to dragons and zombies? To be sure, once Martin decided to go medieval, the elements of fantasy in early English literature—from the dragon in *Beowulf* to the magic in *Sir Gawain and the Green Knight*—spilled into his text.[3] But the Shakespearean context points to another explanation.

In terms of genre, where Martin identified fantasy in the history of the Wars of the Roses, 400 years earlier Shakespeare and his co-authors identified tragedy. Specifically, Shakespeare and company structured the *Henry VI* plays using the tradition of *De Casibus Virorum Illustrium*, "the falls of illustrious men," a literary inheritance from the Middle Ages.[4] The genre peaked at a time of the Black Death when plague killed one-third of the people in Europe. Death was everywhere, and that fact cultivated medieval attitudes about how much humans can control their own destinies. Death could befall even the strongest and nicest people who deserved it least. Thus, the concept of fortune—random chance—came to inform tragedy. Its symbol was the Wheel of Fortune, which just keeps spinning: you might find yourself at the top of the world, a great king or queen enjoying the good life, but just another turn of Fortune's Wheel and you fall from the highest highs to the lowest lows.

In *de casibus* style, the *Henry VI* trilogy is structured as a series of falls. Behind the main plot—the tragedy of Henry VI, which stretches over all three plays—there are four sub-tragedies, each with its own sub-tragedies within it:

The Tragedy of Joan of Arc (*1 Henry VI*)
- The Tragedy of Talbot (*1 Henry VI*, 1.1–4.7)
- The Tragedy of John Talbot the Younger (*1 Henry VI*, 4.7)

The Tragedy of Humphrey, Duke of Gloucester (*1 Henry VI*, 1.1—2 Henry VI*, 4.1)
- The Tragedy of Eleanor (*2 Henry VI*, 1.2–2.4)
- The Tragedy of Winchester (*2 Henry VI*, 3.4)
- The Tragedy of Suffolk (*2 Henry VI*, 4.1)

The Tragedy of Richard, Duke of York (*1 Henry VI*, 2.4—3 Henry VI*, 1.4)
- The Tragedy of Jack Cade (*2 Henry VI*, 4.2–5.1)
- The Tragedy of Old Clifford (*2 Henry VI*, 5.2)

The Tragedy of Richard III (*2 Henry VI*, 5.2—Richard III*)
- The Tragedy of Young Clifford (*3 Henry VI*, 2.6)
- The Tragedy of Somerset (*3 Henry VI*, 5.3)
- The Tragedy of Warwick (*3 Henry VI*, 5.2)
- The Tragedy of Prince Edward (*3 Henry VI*, 5.5)

As a sprawling, episodic, recurring story of one fall after another, there is no protagonist in Shakespeare's first tetralogy. There are no good guys and bad guys, at least not until the very end when Henry VII emerges from the chaos to defeat Richard III, shifting the genre from *de casibus* tragedy to heroic romance. Stated in different terms, the bulk of Shakespeare's first tetralogy tells the story of the Wars of the Roses, but the end suggests the Tudor myth. As a story of good versus evil, the Tudor myth has protagonists and antagonists, which is the key element that led Martin's thoughts on the Tudor myth to the genre of fantasy.

Like the Tudor myth, fantasy literature is about good conquering evil, so it has protagonists and antagonists.[5] The best way to describe the structure of *A Song of Ice and Fire* is not as a series of falls, though the novels certainly retain elements of *de casibus* tragedy. Anyone can die at any moment, and the title sequence of the show evokes *de casibus* tragedy with its spinning astrolabe—a Wheel of Fortune of sorts—and its expansive map that indicates the sprawling, episodic structure of the narrative.[6] It soon becomes clear, however, that Martin structured his narrative around a set of three protagonists. Jon Snow is the protagonist for House Stark, Tyrion for House Lannister, and Daenerys for House Targaryen. Amidst all the minor antagonists to these three heroes, the two major antagonists are Cersei and the White Walkers (which also sounds like the name of a fantastic rock band). Thus, where Shakespeare's first tetralogy has a sprawling episodic structure with an epic feel to it, *A Song of Ice and Fire* has a linear epic structure with an episodic feel. Perhaps the central symbol of Martin's shift from *de casibus* tragedy to historical fantasy comes when one of his heroic protagonists, Daenerys, vows to destroy the Wheel of Fortune:

DAENERYS: Lannister, Targaryen, Baratheon, Stark, Tyrell: they're all just spokes on a wheel. This one's on top, then that one's on top, then on and on it spins.
TYRION: That's a beautiful dream: stopping the wheel. You're not the first person who's ever dreamt it.
DAENERYS: I'm not going to stop the wheel. I'm going to break the wheel.

(5.8)

In sum, Shakespeare identified the formal elements of tragedy in the Wars of the Roses, adding the element of heroic romance in a gesture toward the Tudor myth, while Martin identified the formal elements of fantasy in the Tudor myth, leading him to introduce good guys and bad guys to his fictional medieval history and—much more tangibly—to introduce the elements of fairy tale and fantasy: dragons, zombies, and long-lost princes and princesses. The death and destruction of the Wars of the Roses suggested the genre of *de casibus* tragedy to Shakespeare, whereas the battle between good and evil in the Tudor myth suggested the genre of fantasy to Martin.

And the series' origin in the history of the Tudor myth—rather than the fantasy of Tolkien—may explain why Joseph Young found that Martin has not fundamentally changed the fantasy form.[7] That is not what he set out to do. Fantasy was the means by which Martin radically reimagined historical fiction.

Notes

1 Mikal Gilmore, "George R.R. Martin: The Rolling Stone Interview," *Rolling Stone* (April 23, 2014), https://www.rollingstone.com/culture/culture-news/george-r-r-martin-the-rolling-stone-interview-242487/.
2 Gilmore, "The Rolling Stone Interview."
3 See Carol Parrish Jamison, *Chivalry in Westeros: The Knightly Code of A Song of Ice and Fire* (Jefferson: McFarland, 2018), 25–43.
4 See Paul Budra, *A Mirror for Magistrates and the de casibus Tradition* (Toronto: University of Toronto Press, 2000).
5 See Northrope Frye, *The Secular Scripture: A Study of the Structure of Romance* (Cambridge: Harvard University Press, 1976).
6 I owe this point about the title sequence to Kate Marshall, "Atlas of a Concave World: *Game of Thrones* and the Historical Novel," *Critical Quarterly* 57.1 (2015): 61–70. On the medieval origins of the episodic narrative qualities of *A Song of Ice and Fire*, see *George R.R. Martin's 'A Song of Ice and Fire' and the Medieval Literary Tradition*, ed. Bartłomiej Błaszkiewicz (Warsaw: Warsaw University Press, 2014), esp. Bartłomiej Błaszkiewicz, "George R.R. Martin's A Song of Ice and Fire and the Narrative Conventions of the Interlaced Romance" (15–48), and Rebekah M. Fowler, "Sansa's Songs: The Allegory of Medieval Romance in George R. R. Martin's A Song of Ice and Fire Series" (71–94); Shiloh Carroll, "Chivalric Romance and Anti-Romance," in *The Medievalism of A Song of Ice and Fire and Game of Thrones* (Cambridge: DS Brewer, 2018), 23–53.
7 See Joseph Rex Young, *George R.R. Martin and the Fantasy Form* (New York: Routledge, 2019).

6 Comical-tragical-historical-pastoral
Mixed genre

Several scenes into their tragical history of the Wars of the Roses in *2 Henry VI*, Shakespeare and Marlowe swerved to stage a scene of slapstick comedy: the miracle at St. Albans (2.4). Later in the play, they spent all of Act IV satirizing Jack Cade's rebellion. Why include these scenes of comedy? What is the value of adding comedy to a story that is, in the main, history and tragedy? These scenes aren't just "comic relief" giving audiences a break from the seriousness of the story. They are more substantive, paralleling and commenting upon the main plot.[1] The false miracle at St. Albans contributes to the characterization of King Henry VI as a feckless Christian whose excessive piety weakens how he wields power. Jack Cade's carnivalesque uprising symbolizes the absurdity of the pretenders to the throne in the main plot. In terms of genre, therefore, the *Henry VI* plays tell a "real" story about the past in chronological order, and are thus "history," but they also pull from comedy and tragedy as needed.

There's hardly any comedy at all in *Game of Thrones*. The show has a lot of attitude—hostile irreverence and bad-ass one-liners—but it's a humorless endeavor. At the same time, like Shakespeare's first tetralogy, *Game of Thrones* takes much of its literary energy from its intermingling of genres.

This mixing of genres is more apparent in Martin's books than in the HBO show. The most obvious literary tactic Martin employed in the books is shifting perspectives from chapter to chapter, playing with what narrative theorists call "focalization."[2] An overarching narrative is told in chunks from the situated vantages of individual characters, sometimes leading to questions about the line between narrative fact and character perspective. Shakespeare himself achieved something like this kaleidoscopic view of the main narrative by divvying out soliloquies to create sympathy for competing characters on alternate sides of the conflict. But the less obvious and more powerful literary tactic Martin employed, especially at the start of the first book in the series, was to coordinate shifting character perspectives with shifting literary genres.

The prologue of *A Game of Thrones* starts with horror: action, suspense, and danger out in the wild. "Do the dead frighten you," one character asks (1) shortly before being killed by "the Others" (7) and turning into a zombie. In terms of genre, the horror of the prologue shifts into the heroic romance of the first chapter, which comes from the perspective of Bran Stark, a young boy introduced to heraldry when his father ("He had taken off Father's face, Bran thought, and donned the face of Lord Stark of Winterfell" [12]) invokes his noble authority ("In the name of Robert of the House Baratheon, the First of his Name, King of the Andals and the Rhoynar and the First Men, Lord of the Seven Kingdoms and Protector of the Realm"), sentencing and beheading an "oathbreaker" (13). The third chapter, from Catelyn's perspective, turns to the pastoral mode: "Catelyn had never liked this godswood" (18). The fourth chapter, which narrates upper-class courtship from the perspective of a young female, Daenerys Targaryen, reads like one of Jane Austen's novels of manners: "All that Daenerys wanted was the big house with the red door, the lemon tree outside her window, the childhood she had never known" (26). As *A Game of Thrones* proceeds to bounce from one character to another, and from wilderness to rural to urban settings, these are the four main genres it pulls from.

Shakespeare's penchant for mixing genres was once seen as a blight on his artistic achievement. Samuel Johnson wrote of "the censure which he has incurred by mixing comick and tragick scenes," but defended Shakespeare on grounds of verisimilitude:

> Shakspeare's plays are not in the rigorous and critical sense either tragedies or comedies, but composition of a distinct kind, exhibiting the real state of sublunary nature, which partakes of good and evil, joy and sorrow, mingled with endless variety of proportion and innumerable modes of combination; and expressing the course of the world.[3]

A Song of Ice and Fire belongs to this Shakespearean "distinct kind." While the specifics are vastly different from the mixture of history, tragedy, and comedy in Shakespeare's first tetralogy, *A Song of Ice and Fire*, like Shakespeare's earlier text, draws its literary prowess from generic mixture, not only blending fantasy with history, but also spicing it with horror, romance, pastoral, and the novel of manners.

Notes

1 See Ronald Knowles, "The Farce of History: Miracle, Combat, and Rebellion in 2 *Henry VI*," *The Yearbook of English Studies* 21 (1991): 168–86.
2 See Marc Napolitano, "'Sing for Your Little Life': Story, Discourse and Character," in *Mastering the Game of Thrones: Essays on George R.R. Martin's A Song of Ice and Fire*, ed. Jes Battis and Susan Johnston (Jefferson: McFarland, 2015), 35–56.
3 Samuel Johnson, *Preface to His Edition of Shakespeare's Plays* (London: J. and R. Tonson, et al., 1765), xiii.

7 Narrative relief
From comedy to nudity

Where Shakespeare and his co-authors offered relief from the seriousness of war and politics in scenes of slapstick comedy, HBO offered relief from the political plot of *Game of Thrones* through scenes of gratuitous nudity and sex. According to data collected by Sara David in 2017, more than two-thirds of the episodes of *Game of Thrones* through Season 7 (46 out of 67) feature nudity, overwhelmingly female, most prominently in the first season.[1] From its inception, the show's creators were giddy to be "beyond Rated R" with "a lot of sex."[2] Producers pressured an inexperienced Emilia Clarke into gratuitous nudity, creepily telling her, "You don't want to disappoint your *Game of Thrones* fans."[3] *Game of Thrones* is part of the legacy of "HBO after Dark."[4]

In 2011, the blogger Myles McNutt coined the term *sexposition* to describe the strategy of using nudity and sexuality to enhance scenes of narrative importance, whether to symbolize how sexuality informs character motivations or to keep an audience's attention during long scenes of narration.[5] The showrunners reject this notion. "Personally, I pay less attention to intricate plot points delivered during sex scenes," Benioff said, Weiss adding: "Yes, that's a tricky line to walk. Sex grabs people's attention. But once it has their attention, it tends not to let go of it."[6] Seeing nudity and sex as attention-grabbers, they have also dismissed concerns from critics. "We will address this issue with a 20-minute brothel scene involving a dozen whores, Mord the Jailer, a jackass, and a large honeycomb," Benioff joked during Season 2, Weiss adding:

> There will always be those who want to see less sex, and those who want to see more sex, and those who want to see sex in big tubs of pudding. You just can't please everyone. This year, we're going to focus on the pudding people.[7]

Contra *sexposition*—a clever literary device—sometimes the sex on *Game of Thrones* is about sex. The show especially addresses sexual violence as a reality of war, which George R.R. Martin points out when pressed on the prominence of rape in his series: "Rape and sexual violence have been a part of every war ever fought, from the ancient Sumerians to our present day. To omit them from a narrative centered on war and power would have been fundamentally false and dishonest."[8] At the same time, "there's a Skinemax edge that creeps into *Game of Thrones*," Kate Aurthur writes, noting the show "panders to the *True Blood* audience drunkenly yelling 'boobs!' from the back row."[9] Like that segment of the audience, some of the show's producers beg for more gratuitous nudity on *Game of Thrones*, as recounted by one Season 2 director:

> The weirdest part was when you have one of the exec producers leaning over your shoulder, going, "You can go full frontal, you know. This is television, you can do whatever you want! And do it! I urge you to do it." So I was like, "Okay, well, if you—you're the boss." This particular exec took me to one side and said, "Look, I represent the pervert side of the audience, okay? Everybody else is the serious drama side—I represent the perv side of the audience, and I'm saying I want full frontal nudity in this scene." So you go ahead and do it.[10]

This aspect of the show led Gabrielle Bruny to conclude that "*Game of Thrones*'s treatment of women will tarnish its legacy": "The nudity on *Game of Thrones* was regressive, never equitable and often contrived, and consisted largely of beautiful women dropping trou to titillate the audience, again and again."[11]

"Are the nude scenes in *Game of Thrones* presented as mere pornography, as part of Time Warner and HBO's ploy to attract viewership?" asks Aaron K.H. Ho.[12] He answers *yes*, and Jessica Needham points to the stakes of the "visual misogyny" in the show: "In a world where sexualized advertising and televised female nudity fill our visual mode as a society, this trend points to a problem that is much deeper than *Game of Thrones*."[13]

A comparative analysis with Shakespeare allows us to observe that, between the first tetralogy and *Game of Thrones*, slapstick comedy and gratuitous nudity occupy the same place, structurally, in the logic of these texts. I am not referring to *Game of Thrones*'s explorations of sexual violence, or sexposition, or nudity used for characterization. Those are part of the political plot. But for "the perv side of the audience" the gratuitous nudity in *Game of Thrones* works, surprisingly, much like Shakespearean scenes of slapstick comedy sprinkled into his histories and tragedies. And this parallel creates an opportunity to theorize the concept of *narrative relief* as something different from the more common notion of comic relief.

Giving 1783 as the first recorded instance, the *Oxford English Dictionary* defines *comic relief* as "comic episodes of a play, etc., intended to offset the more serious parts."[14] Humor can be a "pressure valve" for the mind, John Morreall writes.[15] In Shakespeare's first tetralogy and *Game of Thrones*, narrative relief is best understood not in terms of what it is, but in terms of what it is not, namely the serious, usually political, and often tragic main story told.

Serious narratives heavy with politics and ethics elicit a contemplative, reflective, cerebral response from audiences. That is hard mental work which needs alleviation, something that is not the delayed gratification of cogitation but instead instantly pleasurable. A serious text often needs to give its audience what-they-want to cultivate an audience open to receiving what-they-need. Such a text needs something that appeals to the body rather than the mind. Slapstick comedy and gratuitous nudity both appeal to audiences' pleasure centers but are used strategically in Shakespeare's first tetralogy and *Game of Thrones* in the service of the serious narrative. This narrative relief provides alleviation from the seriousness of the main plot, allowing its tensions to reduce to a simmer, preventing an audience from checking out of a self-serious narrative that is all education and no entertainment.

Narrative relief works differently than the comedic parallel or subplot.[16] That comedic parallel is not relief from the main plot of the story. Instead, it focuses an audience's attention on the themes of the main plot, emphasizing and developing them. Given this distinction, I would think of the miracle at St. Albans in *1 Henry VI* as narrative relief, but not Jack Cade's rebellion in *2 Henry VI*. I would think of Osric in Act V of *Hamlet* as narrative relief, but not the gravediggers. As a parody of Prince Hal's actual father, Falstaff is not narrative relief, but Mistress Quickly is. The Porter in *Macbeth* is not narrative relief, but Dogberry in *Much Ado about Nothing* is. The fool in *King Lear* and the comedic subplot in Marlowe's *Doctor Faustus* are not narrative relief, but R2D2 and C3PO in *Star Wars* and the goofball sidekicks in the Disney films are. Beyond comedy, musical numbers in theater and montages in film can be forms of narrative relief, pleasurable interludes allowing audiences to breathe and process. Yet nudity and sexuality in a text like *Fifty Shades of Gray* are not narrative relief: sex is the central focus of the main story.

As Shannon Wells-Lassagne has discussed, sexually explicit material is infused in recent "quality television" far beyond *Game of Thrones*—*Rome*, *True Blood*, *True Detective*, and *Westworld* are only the most prominent examples.[17] That growing trend leaves us with questions both analytical and ethical. How has the rise of premium streaming television—consumed in the privacy of one's own home, in contrast to a public theater—contributed to the rise of nudity as narrative relief? What are the social consequences—the effects on the minds and lives of viewers—of using nudity as a "pressure valve" for narrative? What happens when audiences confuse nudity in scenes of sexual violence for gratuitous nudity meant for narrative relief? What does the overwhelmingly female nudity say about who *Game of Thrones* imagines its audience to be? How do women engage with the nudity in *Game of Thrones*, which hardly feels comparable to, for example, "*Girls'* depictions of the female body as an unruly, unconfined, and dominant space [that] celebrate women's subjectivity."[18] How do straight women, gay men, and asexual people experience the gendered use of female nudity as narrative relief in recent television?

Notes

1 Sara David, "Counting Every Instance of Rape, Death, and Nudity on 'Game of Thrones'," *Vice* (Sept. 7, 2017), https://broadly.vice.com/en_us/article/qvvx83/game-of-thrones-by-the-numbers.
2 Catriona Wightman, "'Game of Thrones' Is 'beyond Rated R'," *HuffPost* (Nov. 1, 2011), https://www.digitalspy.com/tv/ustv/a297256/game-of-thrones-is-beyond-rated-r/.
3 Dax Shepherd, Interview with Emilia Clarke, *Armchair Expert* (Nov. 18, 2019), https://armchairexpertpod.com/pods/emilia-clarke.
4 See Jeffrey P. Jones, "Erotica," in *The Essential HBO Reader*, ed. Gary R. Edgerton and Jeffrey P. Jones (Lexington: University Press of Kentucky, 2008), 274–87.
5 Myles McNutt, "Game of Thrones—'You Win or You Die'," *Cultural Learnings* (May 29, 2011), https://cultural-learnings.com/2011/05/29/game-of-thrones-you-win-or-you-die/.
6 Michael Mechanic, "'Game of Thrones' Has Succeeded Beyond Its Creators' Wildest Dreams," *Mother Jones* (March/April 2013), https://www.motherjones.com/media/2013/03/hbo-game-thrones-season-3-interview-david-benioff-dan-weiss/.
7 Jace Lacob, "David Benioff, D. B. Weiss Discuss 'Game of Thrones' Season 2, More," *The Daily Beast* (Aug. 29, 2011), https://www.thedailybeast.com/david-benioff-d-b-weiss-discuss-game-of-thrones-season-2-more.
8 Dave Itzkoff, "George R.R. Martin on 'Game of Thrones' and Sexual Violence," *New York Times* (May 2014), https://artsbeat.blogs.nytimes.com/2014/05/02/george-r-r-martin-on-game-of-thrones-and-sexual-violence/.

52 *Narrative relief: from comedy to nudity*

9 Kate Aurthur, "9 Ways 'Game of Thrones' Is Actually Feminist," *BuzzFeed* (April 17, 2013), https://www.buzzfeed.com/kateaurthur/9-ways-game-of-thrones-is-actually-feminist.
10 "'Blackwater' Director Neil Marshall on Nudity and Creating the Battle," *Winter Is Coming* (June 6, 2012), https://winteriscoming.net/2012/06/01/blackwater-director-neil-marshall-on-nudity-and-creating-the-battle/.
11 Gabrielle Bruny, "Game of Thrones's Treatment of Women Will Tarnish Its Legacy," *Esquire* (April 11, 2019), https://www.esquire.com/entertainment/tv/a27099255/game-of-thrones-treatment-of-women-controversy-legacy/.
12 Aaron K.H. Ho, "Pornography, Postwoman and Female Nudity," in *Vying for the Iron Throne: Essays on Power, Gender, Death and Performance in HBO's Game of Thrones*, ed. Lindsey Mantoan, Sara Brady (Jefferson: McFarland, 2018), 29.
13 Jessica Kathryn Needham, "Visual Misogyny: An Analysis of Female Sexual Objectification in *Game of Thrones*," *Femspec* 17.2 (2017): 14.
14 "comic, n. and adj.," in *Oxford English Dictionary*, Oxford University, OED Online, special uses, "comic relief n."
15 John Morreall, *Comic Relief: A Comprehensive Philosophy of Humor* (Chichester: Wiley-Blackwell, 2009), 15–23.
16 On these different modes of generic mixing, see Arthur Huntington Nason, "Shakespeare's Use of Comedy in Tragedy," *The Sewanee Review* 14.1 (1906): 28–37; Susan Snyder, *The Comic Matrix of Shakespeare's Tragedies: Romeo and Juliet, Hamlet, Othello, and King Lear* (Princeton: Princeton University Press, 1979).
17 Shannon Wells-Lassagne, "Prurient Pleasures: Adapting Fantasy to HBO," *Journal of Adaptation in Film & Performance* 6.3 (2013): 415–26.
18 Jocelyn L. Baily, "'The Body Police': Lena Dunham, Susan Bordo, and HBO's *Girls*," in *HBO's Girls and the Awkward Politics of Gender, Race, and Privilege*, ed. Elwood Watson, Jennifer Mitchell, and Marc Edward Shaw (Lanham: Lexington, 2015), 29.

8 Spectacle and success from the medieval church service to CGI

Shakespeare's first tetralogy was enormously popular in the Elizabethan age.[1] Those same plays have become some of Shakespeare's least popular plays in the modern age.[2] *A Song of Ice and Fire* was initially only popular with a niche audience in fantasy literature, not with mainstream America.[3] In contrast, the HBO version of *Game of Thrones* was the most popular television show in the world during its run.[4] The popularity of *Game of Thrones* is often associated with the carnal pleasures provided in its gratuitous sex and violence. Looking more closely, however, the examples of Shakespeare's first tetralogy and *Game of Thrones* suggest a theory of literary popularity: literature becomes popular when it exploits the most recent technological advances in spectacle.

First theorized as one of the six elements of drama in Aristotle's *Poetics*, "spectacle" refers to the visual aspect of drama: costume, scenery, gestures, etc.[5] Although Aristotle thought it was the least important element of drama, the power of spectacle can be observed from the very beginning of English drama in the medieval church service. With a largely illiterate laity, clergy found that, instead of reading Bible stories during church, they could spice things up and keep their audience's attention by performing them.[6]

That sort of spectacle was missing, of course, from Shakespeare's sources: the historical writing that emerged in sixteenth-century England. From early Tudor humanist historiographers like John Rous, Robert Fabian, Polydore Vergil, and Thomas More to later professional historians such as Richard Grafton, Edward Hall, Raphael Holinshed, and John Stow, prose histories were popular with elite scholars, but certainly not with the general public. Recalling the medieval mystery plays, the Elizabethan history plays exploited the power of spectacle to educate their audience, only this time in politics rather than religion.[7]

There were some history plays earlier in the sixteenth century—like John Bale's *King Johan* (ca. 1538), Thomas Legge's *Richardus Tertius* (1579), and the anonymous *Famous Victories of Henry V* (ca.1586)—but the Elizabethan history play really came into its own with Marlowe's *Tamburlaine the Great*, a play about the Persian emperor staged in two parts around 1587–88. Near 1589, another anonymous early history play, *The Troublesome Reign of John, King of England*, was performed. In 1590, Marlowe's *Tamburlaine* was published in two parts, creating a market for two-part history plays. Probably written around that time, Shakespeare and Marlowe's *Henry VI* trilogy is filled with spectacle.[8] More than half of the scenes in *1 Henry VI* (26 out of 36) include battles, most memorably those pitting the English general Talbot against the French warrior Joan of Arc. The rest of the trilogy is similarly filled with the Battle of St. Albans (*2 Henry VI*, 5.2), the Battle of Wakefield (*3 Henry VI*, 1.3), the Battle of Towton (*3 Henry VI*, 2.3–5), the Battle of Barnet (*3 Henry VI*, 5.2), and the Battle of Tewkesbury (*3 Henry VI*, 5.3–5). Beyond battle scenes, the *Henry VI* trilogy stages memorable spectacles in the appearance of Joan's fiends (*1 Henry VI*, 5.4.1–29), the conjuring of the spirit Asmath (*2 Henry VI*, 1.4.1–36), and the three suns that appear overhead to the York brothers (*3 Henry VI*, 2.1.25–40).

Spectacle has changed with the times as the medium of English drama developed from the thrust stage of the Elizabethan age to the proscenium theater of the Restoration era to the film screen, the television screen, and the mobile phone screen. Most recently, in contrast to films like the original *Star Wars* trilogy, which used physical models to achieve special effects, computer generated imaging (CGI) has been the frontier in spectacle.[9] In the early 1990s, films like James Cameron's *Terminator 2: Judgment Day* (1991) and Steven Spielberg's *Jurassic Park* (1993) started blending live action with CGI animation effectively. A demand for this kind of spectacle drove major movie events, such as the *Star Wars* prequels (1999–2005), the *Lord of the Rings* trilogy (2001–03), the *Harry Potter* film series (2001–11), and the Marvel Cinematic Universe (2008-Present), totally reorienting Hollywood to center upon the genres of science fiction and fantasy.

But spectacle was missing, of course, from Martin's *A Song of Ice and Fire* novel series. He even, after some bad experiences in Hollywood, sought to make the books "unfilmable."[10] It took the medium of television, the HBO corporation, and an enormous budget to bring Martin's fantasy world to life. According to the *Hollywood Reporter*, producing the pilot cost between $5 and $10 million and, according to Marketplace, the show cost around $6 million per episode in early seasons (contrast that with the $2 million per episode that most cable shows cost).[11] By season six, HBO was spending $10 million per episode. Parts of this budget went to talent and location, but a lot went to spectacle—costumes, sets, and CGI. For instance, the opening scene of *Game of Thrones* required both a massive CGI-created wall of ice and a decapitated head. Much of the first season is filled with striking and expensive visuals, ranging from the lush landscapes of Winterfell and Essos to the ornate castles and costumes of King's Landing. Many of the major moments in the narrative then center upon CGI: Daenerys walking out of the pyre with three CGI baby dragons (1.10), Melisandre giving birth to a shadow that kills Renly Baratheon (2.4), a White Walker riding an undead wight-horse to the elaborately made-up Night King (4.4), aerial shots of sailors arriving at Braavos with its massive statue of a titan standing guard (4.6), Arya gouging out the eyes of Meryn Trant (5.10). Framing shots of CGI crowds mulling about in city streets or CGI caravans traveling across open plains can cost tens of thousands of dollars. And climactic battle scenes such as the Battle of Blackwater Bay (2.9), the Massacre at Hardhome (5.8), the Battle of the Bastards (6.9), the Loot Train Attack (7.4), and the Fall of the Wall (7.6) combine the need for sprawling CGI armies with spectacular CGI renderings of half-decomposed zombies or fire-breathing dragons.

Notes

1 Laura Estill, "Was Shakespeare as Popular in His Own Time as He Is Now?" *British Council* (June 9, 2015), https://www.britishcouncil.org/voices-magazine/was-shakespeare-popular-his-own-time-he-now.
2 Dan Kopf, "What Is Shakespeare's Most Popular Play?" *Priceonomics* (Sept. 22, 2016), https://priceonomics.com/what-is-shakespeares-most-popular-play/.
3 Gerard Hynes, "From Westeros to HBO: George R. R. Martin and the Mainstreaming of Fantasy," in *Twenty-First-Century Popular Fiction*, ed. Bernice M. Murphy and Stephen Matterson (Edinburgh: Edinburgh University Press, 2018): 41–52.
4 Alex Wong, "The 20 Most Popular Shows in the World Right Now," *Inverse* (Oct. 5, 2017), https://www.inverse.com/article/37094-most-popular-tv-shows-right-now-star-trek-game-of-thrones.
5 Aristotle, *Poetics*, trans. Richard Janko (Indianapolis: Hackett, 1987), 1450b.
6 M.D. Anderson, *Drama & Imagery in English Medieval Churches* (Cambridge: Cambridge University Press, 1963).
7 Brian Walsh, *Shakespeare, the Queen's Men, and the Elizabethan Performance of History* (Cambridge: Cambridge University Press, 2009).
8 David Bevington, "Thus Play I in One Person Many People: Performing the Histories," in *This Wide and Universal Theater: Shakespeare in Performance, Then and Now* (Chicago: University of Chicago Press, 2007), 73–104.

9 Stephen Prince, *Digital Visual Effects in Cinema: The Seduction of Reality* (Piscataway: Rutgers University Press, 2012).
10 George R.R. Martin, preface to Bryan Cogman, *Inside HBO's Game of Thrones* (San Francisco: Chronicle, 2012), 5.
11 James Hibberd, "HBO: 'Game of Thrones' Dailies 'look fantastic'," *Hollywood Reporter* (Oct. 30, 2010), https://www.hollywoodreporter.com/live-feed/hbo-game-thrones-dailies-look-52924; Jana Kasperkevic, "Let's Do the Numbers on 'Game of Thrones'," *Marketplace* (July 24, 2017), https://www.marketplace.org/2017/07/21/business/lets-do-numbers-game-thrones.

9 *Game of Thrones* as Shakespearean performance
Interviews with the actors

When you see behind the scenes of *Game of Thrones*, it throws the whole affair into danger. Consider Emelia Clarke as Daenerys Targaryen petting the large, green pillow on the end of a stick to be CGI-ed into one of her dragon's heads (Figure 9.1). It's weird. Seeing the production photographs breaks the dramatic illusion, brings us back to reality, and endangers the audience's engagement with the show. Isn't this all a bit silly when we think about it? Grown men and women dressing up in goofy costumes, pretending to be kings and queens in a magical fantasy land with zombies and fire-breathing dragons? It feels immature, even embarrassing, but *Game of Thrones* works because it represents this wildly improbable alternate reality with utter sincerity and conviction. The show doesn't feel absurd when you're watching it. It's convincing, plausible, even realistic. How do they pull this off?[1]

The stellar acting makes *Game of Thrones* believable, and significantly the cast draws extensively from the world of Shakespearean performance. The list of *Game of Thrones* actors who have played Shakespearean roles is extensive, though this one is not meant to be exhaustive:

- Mark Addy (Robert Baratheon): Dogberry
- Roger Alam (Illyrio Mopatis): Falstaff, Demetrius, Morgan in *All's Well*, Mercutio, Theseus, Oberon, Clarence in *Richard III*, Duke Vincentio, Sir Toby Belch, Brutus, Benedick, Macbeth, Ulysses, Prospero
- Nono Anozie (Xaro Xhoan Daxos): King Lear, Othello, Oberon
- Sean Bean (Eddard Stark): Romeo, Macbeth
- David Bradley (Walder Frey): The Gardener in *Richard II*
- Jim Broadbent (Archmaester Ebrose): Buckingham in *Richard III*, Gloucester in *Lear*
- Tom Brooke (Lothar Frey): Corporeal Nym

58 Game of Thrones, *Shakespearean performance*

Figure 9.1 Emilia Clarke as Daenerys Targaryen, on set with her "dragon." Image from Pixomondo, "Game of Thrones Season 4 Making Of," *YouTube* (Jan. 29, 2015), https://www.youtube.com/watch?v=ssJwFjyS7q8.

- Oona Chaplin (Talisa Stark): Bottom
- Gwendoline Christie (Brienne of Tarth): Lady Macbeth, Queen in *Cymbeline*
- Liam Cunningham (Davos Seaworth): Orlando
- Charles Dance (Tywin Lannister): Henry V, Coriolanus, Fortinbras
- Essie Davis (Lady Crane): Viola, Juliet, Lady Macbeth, Katerina, Jane Shore
- Stephen Dillane (Stannis Baratheon): Hamlet, Macbeth, Prospero, Jacques
- Peter Dinklage (Tyrion Lannister): Richard III
- Natalie Dormer (Margery Tyrell): Adriana
- Richard Dormer (Beric Dondarrion): Angelo
- Michelle Fairley (Catelyn Stark): Emelia, Lady Macbeth, Cassius
- Tara Fitzgerald (Selyse Baratheon): Hermione, Lady Macbeth
- Aidan Gillen (Petyr Baelish): Ariel, Vincentio
- Ian Glen (Jorah Mormont): Hamlet, Aufidius, Macbeth, Edgar, Henry V, Warwick, Kent, Marcus Andronicus
- Julian Glover (Grand Maester Pycelle): King Lear, Albany, Claudius, Gravedigger, Laertes, Macbeth, Jailer, Orsino, Malvolio, Aufidius, Henry IV, Edward IV, Warrick in Henry VI, John of Gaunt, Charles the Wrestler, Tybalt, Friar Lawrence, Prospero, Polixines, Benedict, Don John, Morocco, Montano, Petruchio, King of France in *Henry V*, Buckingham in *Henry VIII*, Caesar, Cassius, Antony, Aaron, Theseus, and Snug the Joiner.

Game of Thrones, *Shakespearean performance* 59

- Richard E. Grant (Izembaro): Andrew Aguecheek
- Conleth Hill (Varys): Macbeth, Bottom, Theseus, Paroles
- Ciarán Hinds (Mance Rayder): Richard III, Achilles, Julius Caesar, Claudius
- Mark Lewis Jones (Shagga): Leontes, Marc Antony, Costard, Lorenzo, Ferdinand, Earl of Richmond
- Ellie Kendrick (Meera Reed): Juliet
- Anton Lesser (Qyburn): Richard III, Hamlet, Bolingbroke, Romeo, Troilus, Edgar, Petruchio, Duke of Exeter
- Harry Lloyd (Viserys): Edmund Mortimer
- Patrick Malahide (Balon Greyjoy): Claudius
- Joseph Mawle (Benjin Stark): Troilus, Leontes
- Ian Mcelhinney (Barristan Selmy): Barnardo
- Tim McInnery (Robert Glover): Iago
- Tobias Menzies (Edmure Tully): Cornwall, Hamlet, Henry V
- Lucian Msamati (Salladhor Saan): Pericles, Iago
- Pedro Pascal (Oberon Martell): Don John, Edmund
- Jonathan Pryce (High Sparrow): Hamlet, Macbeth, King Lear, Shylock, Petruchio, Octavius Caesar, Angelo
- Robert Pugh (Craster): Glendower
- Diana Rigg (Olenna Tyrell): Cordelia, Viola, Lady Macbeth, Helena, Adriana, Regan, Bianca, Lady Macduff
- Clive Russell (Brynden Tully): Edmund, Ajax
- DeObia Sparei (Areo Hotah): Polixines, Hector, Mercutio
- Mark Stanley (Grenn): Brutus
- Donald Sumpter (Maester Luwin): Iachimo, Marcus Andronicus, Orsino, Don John
- Owen Teale (Allister Thorne): Edmund, King of Navarre, Bassanio, Hotspur, Mark Antony, Fluellin
- Natalia Tena (Osha): Desdemona
- Indira Varma (Ellaria Sand): Bianca, Olivia, Tamora
- Miltos Yerolemou (Syrio Forel): The Porter, Puck, Mercutio, Peter in *Romeo and Juliet*, Demetrius, Dromio, Feste, Bottom, Clown in *Othello*

"I've not been in only five of his plays," Glover told me. I interviewed him in the summer of 2018—along with Anton Lesser and Conleth Hill—to ask about acting in Shakespeare, acting in *Game of Thrones*, and the similarities and differences between these two roles.[2]

One theme in these interviews was the repeated claim to treat all roles alike—"I have always approached every role in the same way:

Shakespeare or Beckett or Frayn or Friel or Benioff and Weiss," Hill said—even while enumerating the very real differences between acting in these two spheres. "There are huge differences," Hill later said.

> The play will be rehearsed and performed eight times a week. *Game of Thrones* rehearsals depended on the type of scene, but we usually went through things with the directors and D-and-D [David Benioff and D.B. Weiss] to ensure we were all singing from the same hymn sheet. A typical scene with dialogue would be filmed in a day. The type of work I was lucky enough to do on *Game of Thrones* rarely required lots of rehearsal.

Glover also started his comments with a close association between Shakespearean and *Game of Thrones* roles:

> I hope I approach them all in the same way. You delve into the text; you delve into what you've been provided and try to find out everything you can from the text as given. And you study that text.

Then he concluded ominously, "With Shakespeare, you have to study it intimately." There is a bit more of a game to figure out who Shakespearean characters are—an interpretive puzzle the actor must piece together—than with other characters. "Sometimes you need help to get the stuff out," Glover continued.

> And that's what rehearsals are for, and that's what the other actors are for: to help you, and you help them, to discover actually what Shakespeare intended by this particular scene or this particular play. That's what you do at rehearsals.

As described by these actors, Shakespearean rehearsal often involves an evolving dialog between actor and director, and changes of vision. Sure, Shakespearean directors have their goals, but the actors also hold a great deal of agency in deciding how to bring a character to life. For Lesser,

> Clearly in a rehearsal room over a period of weeks and with a like-minded director who is more interested in a collaborative journey of discovery than in any fixed concept which he is determined to impose from day one, this is a lot easier than in the context of a film, but the principle I find is the same.

Game of Thrones, *Shakespearean performance* 61

With respect to acting, the most obvious separation between Shakespeare and *Game of Thrones* is the divide between stage and screen. "Pretty much everything is brought down in a film," Glover said.

> In the same sort of way, *Game of Thrones* is brought down. Cersei is terribly quiet. Much more quiet than you have to be with Shakespeare, than Margaret has to be. Margaret's cursing in *Henry VI*: big, loud things. And you've got to be able to do that but, at the same time, also be very natural for your film or television show, which is actually something sitting in somebody's living room, a quite different kettle of fish from sitting inside a theater.

Lesser drew attention to physical movement in the two different spheres of acting:

> When I first did television (having started my career steeped in Shakespeare at Stratford) I felt very un-prepared and found the requirement always to "do less" to be very frustrating. I remember a teacher at RADA [Royal Academy of Dramatic Art] actually tying my hands behind my back to stop me waving them around while delivering a speech! But once I accepted that this was a completely different animal, I quickly began to respond to the specific requirements of the medium and to really enjoy it. Once the new set of tools became familiar I could see that the job was essentially always the same: to serve the author's intention by not standing between his work and the audience, but to remain an open channel to reveal it. So in terms of what is different between *Game of Thrones* and a Shakespeare play from this actor's perspective I would say none. My job is the same: does this character I am playing have authenticity? is he (within the world of the piece) a credible human being whose motives and actions we can recognize in ourselves?

After stage versus screen, the next great divide between Shakespeare and *Game of Thrones* is the language. Glover was unflinching about *Game of Thrones*:

> It's not a Shakespearean text. It's written very firmly in prose. None of it's lyrical. None of it's beautiful text. It's damn good text, very strong text, very virile text, very muscular text. But it's not Shakespearean text. It couldn't be without the verse.

To Glover, the verse in Shakespeare's plays is an actor's best friend:

> If you do the verse it sounds much more natural than if you don't. He gives you all the clues of how to say it in his verse. That's the way of going into Shakespeare. You read it as he wrote it because he was an actor himself. He knew the things that helped an actor.

Then he continued, "Of course, you don't have verse in *Game of Thrones*," but hesitated a bit. "I was going to say, 'You don't have that problem,' but actually you don't have that help that the verse gives you." Add to the difference between verse and prose the fact that *Game of Thrones* is a much more visual, much less linguistic, text, and the challenge of conveying character is even greater, as Lesser observed:

> In terms of approaching the character of Qyburn, of course the parameters are smaller and the canvas more limited (instead of soliloquy I was limited to lines like "Yes your grace," and occasionally cryptic comments like "Belief is so often the death of reason," and a whole lot of lurking!) but the challenge is still the same: to find the same depth and complexity with very little to say, and thereby to reveal as much as one can that is true about being a human being—about what Qyburn and Hamlet share.

Preparing for a role in *Game of Thrones*—where there is variously a strict mythology to be served and an open-ended story not yet completed—could feel quite different from the approach actors usually take to Shakespeare. To Glover, however, the rigidity of the confines in *Game of Thrones* actually felt similar to Shakespearean acting:

> When you're on the set, the dialog they've given you—which you've accepted, you've talked about it, of course, before you rehearse it, then you rehearse it, and little changes are made, perhaps, in rehearsal—once you've decided on that text, not one syllable can be changed. And that is the same, of course, with Shakespeare: don't change anything. Sometimes you can get a bit annoyed on the set.

Glover thinks Shakespearean acting is all about negotiating the paradox between a text you must remain absolutely faithful to and a performance where you make a character your own:

> You go to your text; you find out what the author's given you. Sometimes you're able to invest a little something of your own on

top of that. So you try to make it your own. Actually, the way you speak Shakespeare's intentions can vary in many, many ways. That's why we get different performances of Hamlet every time. They may be brilliant performances of Hamlet, absolutely based in the text, but they can be completely different. Otherwise, they wouldn't be plays that can still be performed after 400 years.

Because Shakespearean characters are so deep and open to alternate interpretations, Shakespearean acting is often not about conveying a new story to an audience that has never heard it before as much as it is about revealing new dimensions to well-known characters and stories. An anxiety of influence can emerge, given the great actors who have played the great roles over the centuries, as Lesser explained:

> The approach I personally always try to take is from a position of not knowing, which I suppose ideally is no position at all. By which I mean that I try to be as open and vulnerable as possible, to have no reference to any thoughts about who may have done the part before (and done it "definitively"), to give myself the maximum room for the character to express itself.

In stark contrast to Shakespearean drama, *Game of Thrones* has never been done before. An actor has free rein. And, according to Glover, *Game of Thrones* can't be done again:

> It is a remarkable series, a groundbreaking series which can never be copied. You can't do another *Game of Thrones*. It can't be done. You can repeat *Star Wars*; you can go on doing *Star Wars* forever. But *Game of Thrones* you can't repeat: the whole way they do it, the setting of it, the acting of it, the writing of it. It can't be repeated. So it's a completely unique piece of work.

Whereas Shakespeare is replicable in many different ways—open to modification and repetition with difference—*Game of Thrones* is a one-time artwork, at least to Julian Glover.

All three actors I spoke with saw, in Hill's words, "huge similarities between Shakespeare's brilliant observation of the human condition and that of George R.R. Martin and David and Dan. They're all brilliant observers of the rest of us humans!" As John Bradley, who played Samwell Tarly, wrote in *Inside HBO's Game of Thrones*, "It's like Shakespeare—you can be in huge outrageous places and situations, but it comes down to a deep-rooted understanding of psychology and human situations."³ Glover in particular voiced the ephemeral Shakespearean quality of *Game of Thrones*:

> The extraordinarily convoluted politicizing and physical execution, physical torture, mental torture, and the attempt to claim superiority in the state—that is all the same theme. But I can't see parallels, except in big instances. "Oh, well that was the way they got rid of Richard II, wasn't it?" It's that the whole essence of it is Shakespeare. We know that's the kernel of the series. You sometimes think about that when rehearsing. You say, "Oh my God, that was *Richard III*, wasn't it?" But I couldn't choose a scene from it to say, "That was straight out of *Henry IV, Part II*." I can't pull actual instances out; it's an over-riding thing. When you're thinking about it, and you're doing it, you suddenly say, "Whoa, crikey, that was certainly from *Hamlet*, wasn't it? Well, yes, but that wasn't a history play. No, but it was in *Hamlet*." That sort of thing happens.

During these interviews, the idea that struck me most powerfully was that acting Shakespeare, especially Shakespearean tragedy—those lines written in formal verse, delivered in a high style, talking about important matters of state—prepares one to deliver convincingly the text of *Game of Thrones*. In both cases, the actor must be able to make current and real to a twenty-first-century audience a slice of life as medieval royalty that none of us has experienced, and a world far removed from reality that none of us has ever lived in. "The experience of doing Shakespeare will help you with the very big themes in *Game of Thrones*," said Glover. Shakespearean acting is practice for pretending to be someone very different from who you actually are—often a king or queen or liege to one—and the performance requires you to convey that experience convincingly to an audience that also has no experience with that world—except in the rare case when someone in the audience does know what it's like to be a royal, as in one story Glover told me when describing Shakespeare's ability to inhabit the minds of his characters:

> He just keeps on getting it right. Every time you work on a Shakespeare, you go, "Christ, I did that last week," or, "How did he know how to do that?" How did he get into the head of Cleopatra? How did this 48-year-old man get into Cleopatra's head? You know, I did the *Henry IV* plays at Stratford-Upon-Avon, playing Henry IV, and the Prince of Wales, our Prince of Wales, Prince Charles,

came to see them—he's a great Shakespeare freak—and we were talking together afterwards about it. He said, "Shakespeare's so amazing," and I dutifully said, "Yes, sir, of course, yes indeed." He said, "No, but think about it: if you're Prince of Wales, you're Prince of Wales, or you're king, or you're dead. Nobody else knows what it's like to be Prince of Wales. How is it that Shakespeare got it so right?"

Glover then turned to the value of Shakespearean training for performing "the big moments" in *Game of Thrones*:

> Very big acting, very demonstrative acting—that's almost gone now in methods of acting, not that it isn't sometimes relevant. But enormous acting—which happened at the time of Garrick, and more recently in the times of Olivier, and Gielgud, and Richardson, and people like that, now Ralph Fiennes and Derek Jacobi, people like that, they know exactly when to do the really big stuff. Paul Scofield was a master at it. They know how to do the really big stuff, but not to ever, ever, ever sound unnatural doing it.

Having Shakespearean training gives an actor resources to draw upon that a great actor—but not a Shakespearean actor—might not have available.

Using Shakespearean actors to make the fantastic realistic is not limited to *Game of Thrones*. *Star Wars* works because Shakespearean actors made the mythology believable. This is true for the original trilogy (before he was Darth Vader, James Earl Jones was Othello and King Lear; before he was Obi One Kinobi, Alec Guinness was Hamlet and Richard II), the prequels (Liam Neeson was on stage at the Dublin Shakespeare Theatre Festival before he was Qui-Gon Jinn; Christopher Lee was lurking in the background of Olivier's *Hamlet* [1948] and Burge's *Julius Caesar* [1970] before he was Count Dooku), or the final trilogy (Oscar Issac was Romeo and Proteus before Poe Dameron, and Hamlet afterward; John Boyega was Othello before Finn). Similarly, *Star Trek* was captained by a classically trained Shakespearean actor whether in the original series (William Shatner) or the next generation (Patrick Stewart). The *Lord of the Rings* trilogy relied upon Shakespearean actors for characters both mythical (Ian McKellen and Christopher Lee) and comical (John Rhys-Davies and Ian Holm). Many of the foes and faculty in the *Harry Potter* films were tenured Shakespeareans: Kenneth Branagh, Maggie Smith, Emma Thompson, Ralph Fiennes, Alan Rickman, Helena Bonham

Carter, Michael Gambon, and Brendan Gleeson, among others. And the *X-Men* franchise is helmed by four Macbeths—Patrick Stewart, Ian McKellen, Michael Fassbender, and James McAvoy—aided by a supporting cast of Shakespeareans, including Liev Schreiber (Hamlet before Sabretooth), Alan Cumming (Hamlet before Nightcrawler), and Oscar Isaac (Hamlet before Apocalypse).

Notes

1 For some initial thoughts on *Game of Thrones* from the vantage of Performance Studies, see the "Performance" section in *Vying for the Iron Throne: Essays on Power, Gender, Death and Performance in HBO's Game of Thrones*, ed. Lindsey Mantoan and Sara Brady (Jefferson: McFarland, 2018), 135–212.
2 Quotations in this section come from interviews the author did with Anton Lesser (Aug. 29, 2018), Conleth Hill (Aug. 29, 2018), and Julian Glover (Oct. 1, 2018).
3 John Bradley, quoted in Bryan Cogman, *Inside HBO's Game of Thrones* (San Francisco: Chronicle, 2012), 191.

10 External predictability, internal unpredictability

The human brain likes predictability.[1] That explains, in part, the popularity of genre fiction—detective stories, superhero flicks, and romance novels that satisfyingly follow well-known conventions. As history plays, the popularity of Shakespeare's first tetralogy among its earliest audiences is configured with its predictability, but the popularity of *Game of Thrones* is connected to its unpredictability. Paradoxically, the human brain also likes surprises.[2] But predictability works completely differently with these two texts.

The first tetralogy exhibits an external predictability in which events in the plays are expected because one knows the historical source material upon which they are based. Richard, Duke of York died in real life, in Holinshed's *Chronicles*, and in Shakespeare's first tetralogy (*3 Henry VI*, 1.4.66–108). However surprising it is to the characters in the play that Edward IV marries Elizabeth Woodville, rather than the French Lady Bona, whom he was arranged to marry (*3 Henry VI*, 3.2.37–106), that event is entirely predictable when one knows the history. It seems likely that the predictability of the first tetralogy—most especially its teleological movement toward the Tudor dynasty its original audiences were living under—contributed to its massive popularity in the early-modern age. If so, however, it is also possible that the first tetralogy later became unpopular because the modern age came to value unpredictability over predictability— came to value the "orderly disorder" N. Katherine Hayles associates with postmodernism.[3]

Those same modern values led to the popularity of *Game of Thrones*, but here the unpredictability of the narrative is internal rather than external. When the frame of reference is not historical source material but rather the events of the story in the text, what happens in *Game of Thrones* is highly unpredictable. Eddard Stark's death (1.9) is the most obvious example of an unpredictable plot point. No one saw it coming although, if one is familiar with the Wars of the Roses upon which *A Song of Ice and Fire* was modeled—that is, if the frame of reference for predictability were external rather than internal—Eddard's death would be entirely expected. Robb Stark and Talisa Maegyr's marriage (2.3) is an unpredictable plot twist in light of his betrothal to one of Walder Frey's daughters or granddaughters. Yet Robb and Talisa's marriage is predictable when the frame of reference is external—when one knows the episode is based on Edward IV and Elizabeth Woodville's marriage. Many of the events in *Game of Thrones* are predictable when one knows the historical material upon which they are based but, since the vast majority of its audience is unaware of its historical source material—or those analogs are only identifiable retrospectively—the dominant criteria of predictability is internal rather than external. Thus, the Red Wedding (3.9) was highly unpredictable, both externally speaking, because it did not follow the historical analogy from the Wars of the Roses, and internally speaking, because it eliminated several of the main characters from the narrative. By the time of Jon Snow's death (5.10), it was predictable, given the internal convention of *A Song of Ice and Fire* to kill off main characters. It was *un*predictable to bring Jon Snow back to life, although that resurrection was predictable if one knows the Wars of the Roses and understands how Martin used that source material to structure Jon Snow as the Henry VII of his text—in other words, if the frame of reference is external.

Notes

1 Gregory S. Berns, "Predictability Modulates Human Brain Response to Reward," *Journal of Neuroscience* 21.8 (2001): 2793–98.
2 Tania Luna and LeeAnn Renninger, *Surprise: Embrace the Unpredictable and Engineer the Unexpected* (New York: Perigee, 2015).
3 N. Katherine Hayles, *Chaos Bound: Orderly Disorder in Contemporary Literature and Science* (Ithaca: Cornell University Press, 2018).

11 Eddard as Gloucester
De Casibus Virorum Illustrium

One moment more than any other propelled *Game of Thrones* to the center of conversation in American culture: the execution of Eddard Stark.[1] In American television, you just don't kill off your protagonist at the end of the first season, especially when he's portrayed by Sean Bean, the only actor on the show with a recognizable name. If you knew that Martin modeled *Game of Thrones* on the Wars of the Roses, however, you knew that Eddard was going to die. Once the analogy between Lancasters and Lannisters, Yorks and Starks is recognized, the shared fate of Eddard and Richard, Duke of York is not so surprising after all. In a noteworthy refraction, *The Hollow Crown*—a prominent BBC production of Shakespeare's history plays with a *Game of Thrones* vibe—deliberately recalled the most memorable shot from the first season of *Game of Thrones*, Ned's head on a stake, in a shot of Richard's head (see Figures 11.1 and 11.2).

Figure 11.1 Visual effect of Ned Stark's head on a spike in *Game of Thrones* (1.10).

70 *Eddard as Gloucester*

Figure 11.2 Visual effect of Richard, Duke of York's head on a spike in *The Hollow Crown: The Wars of the Roses*, dir. Dominic Cooke (BBC, 2016). Episode 2.

Both Richard and Eddard are heads of noble households swallowed up in feuding factions and ultimately executed by their rivals. As represented by Shakespeare, however, Richard, Duke of York doesn't really resemble Eddard Stark at all. In Shakespeare's first tetralogy, Richard is characterized by his hereditary claim to the throne (*1 Henry VI*, 2.5.63–92), his military leadership during the war against France (Acts IV and V of *1 Henry VI*) and later the Wars of the Roses (Act V of *2 Henry VI* and Act I of *3 Henry VI*), his cruelty toward Joan of Arc (*1 Henry VI*, 5.5.1–15), his ambition for the English crown (*2 Henry VI*, 1.1.210–55), and his eventual rebellion against Henry VI (*2 Henry VI*, 5.1). None of this sounds like Eddard Stark, the honorable advisor to the king tragically swallowed up in a swamp of courtly corruption in *Game of Thrones*.

In Shakespeare's *Henry VI* trilogy, that role is played by Humphrey, Duke of Gloucester.[2] Gloucester becomes the lord protector when his brother, Henry V, dies young and his infant nephew, Henry VI, is crowned king (*1 Henry VI*, 1.1.37). In *1 Henry VI*, Gloucester is primarily characterized through his bickering with Bishop Winchester (1.1.28–44, 4.1.182–94). Where Winchester is petty and power hungry ("I'll either make thee stoop and bend thy knee," Winchester says of Gloucester, "Or sack this country with a mutiny" [*1 Henry VI*, 5.2.61–62]), Gloucester is said to be "the map of honour, truth, and loyalty" (*2 Henry VI*, 3.1.203). Gloucester then becomes the hapless victim of a conspiracy against him by enemies. Queen Margaret and some of her inner-circle, including the man she is having an affair with, conspire to take away the honorable and well-intentioned Gloucester's advisory position, and then have him killed (*2 Henry VI*, 3.1.233–80). Now, *that* sounds like Eddard Stark.

Like Gloucester, Eddard is not ambitious: he refused to seize the iron throne for himself when he had the chance (1.7). Eddard is also humble and courteous: "I am not worthy of the honor," he tells King Robert Baratheon when Robert asks him to become Hand of the King (1.1). Upon Robert's untimely death, Eddard is, like Gloucester, named lord protector over a child king (1.7). Unlike the ambitious Richard, Duke of York, both Gloucester and Eddard are honorable counselors in the good favor of their kings who are plotted against and killed through the "back-stabbing and scheming and arse-licking" (1.5) of rival counselors.[3]

Shakespeare's first tetralogy attached counselor in-fighting and the downfall of the honorable advisor to the ineptitude of the ruling power.[4] On the one hand, the Duke of Exeter (a choral voice who interprets much of the drama for the audience) presents factional feuding as a disease killing the English nobility from within: "As festered members rot but by degree / Till bones and flesh and sinews fall away, / So will this base and envious discord breed" (*1 Henry VI*, 3.1.191–93). On the other hand, Exeter also presents factionalism as an outgrowth of the child king:

> This jarring discord of nobility,
> This shouldering of each other in the court,
> This factious bandying of their favourites...
> 'Tis much, when sceptres are in children's hands,
> But more, when envy breeds unkind division:
> There comes the ruin, there begins confusion.
> (*1 Henry VI*, 4.1.188–94)

A child, obnoxiously saintly, kind-hearted but weak-willed, Henry VI is no match for the power-hungry adults around him. The whole point of the *Henry VI* trilogy is that the lack of strong leadership in a government where power is centralized—variously presented as the child king who needs babysitting (*1 Henry VI*, 1.1.167–77), the weak king whose excessive piety prevents him from exercising power (*3 Henry VI*, 1.1.226–56), and the mad king who would rather be shepherd than sovereign (*3 Henry VI*, 2.5.1–55)—spawns discord and in-fighting among nobles.

In *Game of Thrones*, the weak king appears, initially, in the form of the philandering Robert Baratheon, who would rather drink and chase women than govern. After Robert's death, a child king emerges, Joffrey Baratheon (1.7). Characterized early in the series as arrogant, petulant, and entitled, Joffrey becomes violent, sadistic, and uncontrollable upon his ascension (2.1). "We've had vicious kings and we've had idiot kings," Tyrion says of his nephew Joffrey, "But I don't know if we've ever been cursed with a vicious idiot boy king" (2.6). Distrust and factionalism plague Joffrey's reign until political backstabbing consumes him and he is poisoned on his wedding day (4.2). Chaos ruled because Joffrey was a morally weak king. His successor—his brother, Tommen, a second child king—more exactly recalls Shakespeare's Henry VI, sensible and well-intentioned but ineffective at exercising power (4.4): he is not morally weak but politically weak. Division and rancor continue, ultimately ending in tragedy when Cersei blows up the Great Sept of Baelor and everyone inside it, including many of the King's council (6.10). Tommen commits suicide (6.10). But this is not the medieval Wheel of Fortune randomly dealing out tragedy. Instead, in both Shakespeare's *Henry VI* and *Game of Thrones*, the council exhibits discord, inefficiency, and downfall specifically because, in a governmental system where power is centralized in one person, a king who is weak—either morally or politically—and cannot wield power effectively creates competition, in-fighting, and backstabbing among the advisory council.

The phenomenon remains with us today: there are strong connections among political inexperience, bureaucratic incompetence in a head of state, counselor in-fighting, and high turnover in government employees. "I think Joffrey is now the king in America," Martin said in 2017. "And he's grown up just as petulant and irrational as he was when he was thirteen in the books."[5] President Donald Trump's administration is only the most obvious case in which a child king—often weak, sometimes crazy—in charge of a government with centralized power creates both factionalism and the fall of honorable advisors.[6] I am not alluding to the dismissals of Trump favorites such as Steve Bannon, Michael Flynn, and Anthony Scaramucci, who play the role of evil henchman more than that of honorable advisor. But the firings of Sally Yates, James Comey, and Marie Yovanovitch show what happens to "honour, truth, and loyalty" when "envy breeds unkind division" because "scepters are in children's hands."

Notes

1 For a reading of Eddard in the context of classical tragedy, see Christopher C. Kirby, "Ned Stark: One Man in Ten Thousand," in *The Ultimate Game of Thrones and Philosophy: You Think or Die*, ed. Eric J. Silverman and Robert Arp (Chicago: Open Court, 2017), 11–18.
2 See Michael Manheim, "Duke Humphrey and the Machiavels," *The American Benedictine Review* 23 (1972): 249–57.
3 As with Shakespeare's first tetralogy, the political backstabbing in *Game of Thrones* is often discussed in the vocabulary of Machiavellianism. See David Hahn, "The Death of Lord Stark: The Perils of Idealism," in *Game of Thrones and Philosophy: Logic Cuts Deeper than Swords*, ed. Henry Jacoby (Hoboken: Wiley, 2012), 75–86; Marcus Schulzke, "Playing the Game of Thrones: Some Lessons from Machiavelli," in *Game of Thrones and Philosophy*, 33–48; William P. MacNeil, "Machiavellian Fantasy and the Game of Laws," *Critical Quarterly* 57.1 (2015): 34–48; Elizabeth Beaton, "Female Machiavellians in Westeros," in *Women of Ice and Fire: Gender Game of Thrones, and Multiple Media Engagements*, ed. Anne Gjelsvik and Rikke Schubart (London: Bloomsbury, 2016), 193–218; Jacopo della Quercia, "A Machiavellian Discourse on *Game of Thrones*," in *Game of Thrones versus History: Written in Blood*, ed. Brian Pavlac (Hoboken: Wiley Blackwell, 2017), 33–46; and Wolfgang Muno, "'Winter Is Coming?' *Game of Thrones* and Realist Thinking," in *The Interplay Between Political Theory and Movies: Bridging Two Worlds*, ed. Ulrich Hamenstädt (Heidelberg: Springer 2019): 135–49.
4 See Joseph Campana, "The Child's Two Bodies: Shakespeare, Sovereignty, and the End of Succession," *English Literary History* 81.3 (2014): 811–39.
5 George R.R. Martin, quoted in Logan Hill, "Kit Harington Already Died Once," *Esquire* (May 24, 2017), https://www.esquire.com/entertainment/a55226/kit-harington-after-game-of-thrones/.
6 See Denise Lu and Karen Yourish, "Hired and Fired: The Unprecedented Turnover of the Trump Administration," *The New York Times* (April 12, 2018), https://www.nytimes.com/interactive/2018/03/16/us/politics/all-the-major-firings-and-resignations-in-trump-administration.html.

12 Wars of roses
A literary trope in social life

The 2016 US presidential election returned time and again to a trope familiar to anyone who studies group dynamics.[1] First, while the massive field of 15 establishment Republican candidates bickered among themselves during the primary election, an outsider with no experience in politics, Donald Trump, swept in to secure the nomination for the Republican ticket. Second, during the general election, as the Democratic Party internally debated if Hillary Clinton was liberal enough, Trump stormed his way to an electoral college victory and the White House. Third, as Clinton-supporting Democrats and Trump-loving Republicans engaged in a bitter and fractious culture war, Russian agents were able to infiltrate the political discourse in America, securing their candidate of choice, leading to a lessening of America's role as the leader of the world.

It was a real-life game of thrones in a twenty-first-century democracy and, if we turn from this social phenomenon to the literary explorations of it in *Game of Thrones* and, before it, Shakespeare's first tetralogy, we can gain a deeper understanding of the trope. We can theorize outward from the Wars of the Roses, the specific historical event, to a generalizable sociological concept. In other words, by structuring its plot on the Wars of the Roses, but detaching that event from its historical moment, *Game of Thrones* helps us theorize what a "war of roses" is: the fractious squabbling that occurs among competing leaders within a group, sewing discord and division, weakening solidarity and defenses against outside forces, allowing those foreign powers to overtake the divided group with relative ease as it gnaws away at itself.

That is, more or less, the thesis of Shakespeare's *Henry VI* trilogy. The internal dispute is between the Lancasters and the Yorks, as memorably illustrated in the temple garden scene of *1 Henry VI*, where the Duke of Somerset tells everyone aligned with the House of Lancaster to pluck a red rose with him, while Richard Plantagenet, who will soon become the Duke of York, asks those who support his claim to the throne to pluck a white rose for the House of York. Richard is right when he says he will carry this dispute to his death:

> And by my soul, this pale and angry rose,
> As cognizance of my blood-drinking hate,
> Will I forever, and my faction, wear
> Until it wither with me to my grave.
> (2.4.107–10)

While the most obvious imagery here associates the roses with the English houses, Shakespeare also attached that imagery to decay and death. Wars of roses end up in tragedy, as the Earl of Warwick prophesies: "I dare say / This quarrel will drink blood another day" (2.4.133–34).

First, these "factious emulations" (*1 Henry VI*, 4.1.113) spill over into supporters of Somerset and York, two underlings named Bassett and Vernon. King Henry is the one to recognize this internal squabbling as a problem for the foreign war against France:

> If they perceive dissension in our looks,
> And that within ourselves we disagree,
> How will their grudging stomachs be provoked
> To wilful disobedience, and rebel!
> Beside, what infamy will there arise
> When foreign princes shall be certified
> That for a toy, a thing of no regard,
> King Henry's peers and chief nobility
> Destroyed themselves and lost the realm of France!
> (4.1.139–47)

Henry's admonitions are not enough to solidify Somerset and York behind a common cause. When they are assigned to join the English general Talbot in battle against the French, "that villain Somerset" (4.3.9) promises to send troops to help, but reneges because of his petty feud with York, leaving Talbot in the lurch. The battle is a major loss for the English, and here Sir William Lucy is the one to recognize that the internal civil war weakened the English in their external foreign war:

> The fraud of England, not the force of France,
> Hath now entrapped the noble-minded Talbot....
> Whiles they each other cross,
> Lives, honours, lands, and all hurry to loss.
> (4.3.36–53)

76 *Wars of roses*

Add to this conflict between the Lancasters and the Yorks the conflict within the House of Lancaster—epitomized in the rivalry between the Duke of Gloucester and the Bishop of Winchester—and you see why King Henry is so worried that "Civil dissension is a viperous worm / That gnaws the bowels of the commonwealth" (*1 Henry VI*, 3.1.71–73). As noted in the last section, Henry's uncle, the Duke of Exeter, is the one to recognize how these internal disputes will metastasize, bringing defeat in the foreign war against France:

> This late dissension grown betwixt the peers
> Burns under feignèd ashes of forged love,
> And will at last break out into a flame.
> As festered members rot but by degree
> Till bones and flesh and sinews fall away,
> So will this base and envious discord breed.
> And now I fear that fatal prophecy
> Which, in the time of Henry named the Fifth,
> Was in the mouth of every sucking babe:
> That 'Henry born at Monmouth should win all,
> And Henry born at Windsor should lose all.
>
> (3.1.188–98)

In *2 Henry VI*, after the war with France has been lost, and the battle lines are redrawn according to the rapidly mounting civil war, it is those internal tensions within the House of Lancaster that allow the House of York to overtake it. First, Margaret, Suffolk, Winchester, and York conspire to murder Gloucester (3.1). As a result, Suffolk is exiled (3.3) and murdered (4.1), Margaret becomes estranged from her husband (3.3), and Winchester dies of a guilty conscience (3.4). This civil discord then becomes the basis for Richard, Duke of York's decision to assert—finally—his claim to the throne. Punctuating the point in *Richard III*, Shakespeare showed how the internal squabbling within the now-empowered House of York leads to its weakened defenses against a new external threat, the Earl of Richmond and the mounting House of Tudor.

As much as *Game of Thrones* adapts certain character types from Shakespeare's first tetralogy, it adapts the plot typology I have been describing: a war of roses in which power disputes within groups make them vulnerable to conquest from external enemies. In Season 1, this dynamic emerges in the conflict between the Starks and the Lannisters, which threatens to make all of Westeros vulnerable to conquest by the Targaryens. That's why King Robert frets over the fractious and disjointed state of Westeros when telling Cersei that one is a bigger number than five:

> One army—a real army. United behind one leader with one purpose. Our purpose died with the Mad King. Now we've got as many armies as there are men with gold in their purse. And everybody wants something different. Your father wants to own the world. Ned Stark wants to run away and bury his head in the snow. We haven't had a real fight in nine years. Backstabbing doesn't prepare you for a fight and that's all the realm is now—backstabbing and scheming and arse-licking and money-grubbing. Sometimes I don't know what holds it all together.
>
> (1.5)

As the story unfolds, *Game of Thrones* presents one war of roses after another. Civil war breaks out between the Lannisters and the Baratheons, each house having to negotiate that external fight amidst its own internal tensions (between Tyrion and Cersei, e.g., or Stannis and Renly). Meanwhile, two additional wars of roses break out. First, as Daenerys negotiates her family dispute with Viserys, she must also manage her external conflicts with the Dothraki and, as the story continues, a series of outside cities and groups in Essos. Second, as Jon Snow negotiates the inter-group politics of the Night's Watch, he must also manage the external conflict with the Wildings. In each case, whoever is able to maintain group solidarity emerges victorious.

And all of these wars of roses unfold in the context of the overarching existential war of roses between the living and the dead. This plot structure was first made explicit at the end of Season 1, after Ned Stark's execution, when Jon Snow plans to leave the Night's Watch to join the game of thrones, but Jeor Mormont tells him to focus on the conflict that really matters: "Do you think your brother's war is more important than ours?... When dead men and worse come hunting for us in the night, do you think it matters who sits on the iron throne?" (1.10). As the narrative nears its conclusion, the central questions are these: *Which house will survive its inner turmoil to secure the iron throne? And will these competing houses, despite that competition, be able to unify in a common cause against the White Walkers?* Carrying the banner of this top-level war of roses has been the Night's Watch, as Davos told Lyanna Mormont when trying to unite the houses of the north: "Jeor Mormont and Jon Snow both understood that the real war isn't between a few squabbling houses. It's between the living and the dead. And make no mistake, my lady: the dead are coming" (6.7).

Soon after, Davos made the same point to Daenerys: "If we don't put aside our enmities and band together we will die. And then it doesn't matter whose skeleton sits on the Iron Throne" (7.3). In the later seasons of the show, ceasing hostilities between feuding noble houses to unite them against the external threat became Jon Snow's *raison d'être*:

> The long night is coming, and the dead come with it. No clan can stop them, the free folk can't stop them, the Night's Watch can't stop them and all the southern kings can't stop them. Only together, all of us.
> (5.7)

Thus, Jon pleads for unity to both Daenerys ("You'll be ruling over a graveyard if we don't defeat the Night King" [7.3]) and Cersei ("There is only one war that matters. The Great War. And it is here" [7.7]).

In contrast to *the* Wars of the Roses, the fifteenth-century historical event, *a* war of roses is a non-specific occurrence—whether a literary trope with a certain plot structure or a social phenomenon with a certain group dynamic—where internal squabbling within a group weakens its solidarity and defenses, allowing a hostile foreign entity to conquer it easily. Nobles inside the group, who should be friends, start competing for power, fighting for an iron throne. Internal tension, debate, and dispute become fractious in-fighting when people start picking white roses or red. These squabbling houses take their factions to their graves. The quarrel drinks blood. Back-stabbing, scheming, arse-licking, and money-grabbing emerge, along with division, dissent, and discord. These viperous worms gnaw the bowels of the group. The festering body rots away. This loss of solidarity creates weakened defenses when the Great War comes: the only war that really matters. No one clan in the group is strong enough to stop the outside enemies who hear of its vulnerability. The divided group is easily conquered, taken down by the fraud within, not the force outside. Now it doesn't matter whose skeleton sits on the iron throne: "Whiles they each other cross, / Lives, honours, lands, and all hurry to loss." And insofar as the tragic logic of wars of roses is one of the central points of emphasis in *Game of Thrones*, Cersei is profoundly wrong when she utters the line that gives the narrative its name: "When you play the game of thrones, you win or you die; there is no middle ground" (1.7). Being able to live in the middle ground between unity and division is precisely what prevents wars of roses.

Note

1 See Françoise Boucek, *Factional Politics: How Dominant Parties Implode or Stabilize* (New York: Palgrave Macmillan, 2012).

13 The stigmatized protagonist
The tragic model and the heroic model

Halfway through *3 Henry VI*, Richard—Duke of Gloucester, future King Richard III, but up to this point a seemingly minor character—turns to the audience and starts speaking to us directly, explaining the pain and suffering of being physically deformed, and also his ambition for the crown and his plots against his own family (3.2.153–71). Richard was the most demonized historical figure in Shakespeare's England. But here and in later soliloquies (*3 Henry VI*, 5.6.68–94; *Richard III*, 1.1.1–28), Shakespeare framed Richard's villainy with his struggle with physical deformity, leading us to sympathize with a villain we would usually abhor. It would be like someone today telling the story of World War II from Hitler's point of view, asking us to see it from his perspective, asking us to sympathize with him. Add to this sympathy the admiration we have for Richard, who refuses to let his situation in life dictate his destiny, even though he does horrible things to achieve it, as well as the naughty excitement we take from Richard's wicked energy, and we've got Shakespeare's first truly great character, as well as the central interpretive question of the first tetralogy: How do we handle the emergence of a protagonist who is also a villain?[1]

With Richard III, Shakespeare invented the stigmatized protagonist: the central figure whose character and plot are closely bound up with his or her negotiation of negative social attitudes heaped upon him or her in response to some innate aspect of his or her identity (1) that he or she has no control over, but (2) that has come to signify illegitimacy.[2] The stigmatized protagonist was probably the most important literary trope George R.R. Martin inherited from Shakespeare when he wrote *A Song of Ice and Fire*, but Martin adapted the character in two ways.

First, Martin disseminated the stigmatized protagonist to his three main characters: Jon Snow, treated poorly because he is a bastard; Tyrion Lannister, treated poorly because he is a dwarf; and Daenerys

Targaryen, treated poorly because she is a woman. As this paradigm suggests, stigmatized characters face similar situations in life even if they are stigmatized for different reasons, an idea made explicit when Tyrion says to Jon Snow, "All dwarfs are bastards in their father's eyes" (1.1). This extrapolation of the stigmatized protagonist to multiple characters speaks to the increased prominence of stigma as a social problem in the modern world, and the increased prominence of stigma as a literary device for characterization in modern literature.[3]

Second, Martin shifted the genre of stigma. Shakespeare's Richard III exhibits a tragic model of stigma. His physical deformity is said to symbolize his moral villainy, and his resentment toward this treatment spurs his anger, hatred, and hostility toward others, leading to conflict and ultimately catastrophe. Martin shifted the stigmatized protagonist from a tragic model involving villainy and death to a heroic model in which the character's experience with stigma strengthens his or her personality, leading to an "overcoming narrative" and a happy ending.[4] Martin himself seems to agree with Tyrion: "I have a tender spot in my heart for cripples, bastards, and broken things" (1.4).

Jon Snow's story begins when he, a bastard brought home from war to his noble father's household, is denied a seat at the dinner table when the king's family visits—an outsider in a world obsessed with filiation.[5] Where Shakespeare's Richard is the York brother who stands furthest from the crown, Martin's Jon Snow is the Stark brother most removed from the family's inheritance, but Jon is no villain like Richard. He is, to Evan Rosa, "the moral light for redemption in the *Game of Thrones* world."[6] The heroic model of stigma immediately surfaces in a conversation with Tyrion, who knows about being an outsider: "Let me give you some advice, bastard. Never forget what you are. The rest of the world will not. Wear it like armor, and it can never be used to hurt you" (1.1). Deciding that the politics of nobility are not for him, John leaves his house to join the Night's Watch: "No bastard was ever refused a seat there," Jon's uncle, a Night's Watchman tells him about the Wall (1.1). In the Watch, Tyrion tells Jon, "You discard your old family and get a new one" (1.2). Battling against the White Walkers in the north, Jon's talents, bravery, honor, and determination lift him through the ranks of the Night's Watch; he eventually becomes Lord Commander (5.2). He then leads an army south to reclaim Winterfell, the home he once ran away from (6.9). The bastard who once wanted nothing to do with the politics of Westeros is then proclaimed the King in the North (6.10). Where Richard turned from stigma to villainy and ultimately suffered tragedy, Jon works through stigma to heroism and survives the narrative.

Tyron Lannister—called "the imp" in hushed tones at the start of the story (1.1)—is physically deformed like Richard III.[7] Peter Dinklage, who plays Tyrion, portrayed Shakespeare's Richard III a few years before shooting *Game of Thrones*.[8] Both have faced denigration their whole lives: in one of his first scenes, Richard is called a "heap of wrath, foul indigested lump, / As crooked in [his] manners as [his] shape" (*2 Henry VI*, 5.1.157–58), and Tyrion's early life was filled with not-so-subtle belittlement and hostility from his family. "Do you remember, back when you ripped my mother open on your way out of her and she bled to death," Tyrion's sister Cersei asks him: "Mother gone, for the sake of you. There's no bigger joke in the world than that" (2.2). Similarly, Tyrion's father, Tywin, sees his son as "a stunted fool" (1.10) and an "ill-made, spiteful little creature" (3.1). Born deformed into a noble household, both Richard and Tyrion respond to their lack of traditional heroic qualities—strength, bravery, and honor—by developing intellectual virtues. Like Richard, Tyrion is witty, irreverent, and more intelligent than the honorable, able-bodied noblemen around him: "Look at me and tell me what you see," he says to Jon Snow.

> What you see is a dwarf. If I had been born a peasant, they might have left me out in the woods to die. Alas, I was born a Lannister of Casterly Rock. Things are expected of me…. My brother has his sword, and I have my mind. A mind needs books like a sword needs a whetstone.
>
> (1.2)

But Tyrion and Richard diverge on two key points.

First, Tyrion does not share Richard's sexual frustration. On the contrary, Tyrion is a sexual dynamo known for his love of prostitutes and initially described as "a drunken little lecher, prone to all manners of perversion" (1.1). Thus, where Richard "play[s] the devil" (*Richard III*, 1.3.337), Tyrion becomes the "god of tits and wine" (7.5). Audiences later learn that, when he was a young man, Tyrion and his brother Jamie saved a peasant girl being attacked on the side of a road; Tyrion fell in love with her, and they married (1.9). When Tyrion's father found out, he had Jamie tell Tyrion that the girl was a hired prostitute, that the whole road-side episode was staged to make the dwarfish Tyrion feel like a man. Tywin then had Tyrion's wife raped repeatedly, last of all by Tyrion himself. This traumatizing episode, rather than his physical deformity *per se*, is what generates Tyrion's disregard for romantic love and predilection for prostitutes.

When Tyrion later finds out that his wife actually wasn't a prostitute—that their love was real, and Tywin only invented the story to undo his noble son's marriage to a commoner (*SoS* 77)—Tyrion's revenge against his father sparks his progression toward his second major difference from Shakespeare's Richard III. After murdering his father and fleeing his family (4.10), Tyrion gradually shifts from drinking, whoring, and cynicism to serving as a sober and passionate supporter, aide, and advisor to Daenerys Targaryen's campaign.[9] "I've been a cynic for as long as I can remember," he tells her.

> Everyone's always asking me to believe in things: family, gods, kings, myself. It was often tempting until I saw where belief got people. So I said "no thank you" to belief. And yet here I am. I believe in you.
>
> (6.10)

Daenerys herself started out stigmatized as a woman in an oppressive system of patriarchy. She is a slouching, meek girl at the beginning of the narrative (1.1), having been abused, objectified, condescended to by her royal brother, and then treated like chattel, married off against her will, and (in the show) raped by her new husband. Those are the forces descending upon Daenerys, established at the very start of her story, which she overcomes as she ascends from stigma to heroism, beginning in the second episode of the show. Rather than be raped like an animal again by her husband, Daenerys resists him, asserts her autonomy, and impresses him by assuming the dominant sexual position and climbing on top of him in bed (1.2). As she progresses, Daenerys is continually called a "slut" (1.3), "foreign whore" (1.8), and "dumb bitch" (3.1), but she embraces her newfound power as *kaleesi*, gains in confidence and independence, learns that she is magically immune to fire, acquires three dragons (a traditional symbol of heroes), becomes the leader of the Dothraki, acquires an army, builds a trusted council, goes from city to city liberating slaves, earning their trust, building her reputation, and learning to govern, eventually acquiring a fleet of ships and sailing her army to Westeros to reclaim her title. Thus, to critics like Rikke Schubart, Daenerys is a "postfeminist" hero who "is not determined (for instance by a patriarchal society), but can choose her actions."[10] As Daenerys says to Jon Snow—one stigmatized protagonist to another—her story started in stigma and subjugation but veers toward prosperity and heroism:

> I have been sold like a brood mare. I've been chained and betrayed, raped and defiled. Do you know what kept me standing

all those years in exile? Faith. Not in any gods, not in myths and legends. In myself. In Daenerys Targaryen! The world hadn't seen a dragon in centuries until my children were born. The Dothraki hadn't crossed the sea, any sea; they did for me. I was born to rule the Seven Kingdoms, and I will.

(7.3)

Notes

1 See Joel Elliot Slotkin, "Honeyed Toads: Sinister Aesthetics in Shakespeare's *Richard III*," *Journal for Early Modern Cultural Studies* 7.1 (2007): 5–32.
2 See Jeffrey R. Wilson, "The Figure of Stigma in Shakespeare's Drama," *Genre* 51.3 (2018): 237–66.
3 On the social problem, see Erving Goffman, *Stigma: Notes on the Management of Spoiled Identity* (Englewood Cliffs: Prentice-Hall, 1963). On the literary device, see Toni Morrison, *The Origin of Others* (Cambridge: Harvard University Press, 2017).
4 On "overcoming narratives" see, for example, Tanya Titchkosky, "Overcoming: Abled-Disabled and Other Acts of Normative Violence," in *Reading and Writing Disability Differently: The Textured Life of Embodiment* (Toronto: University of Toronto Press, 2007), 177–208.
5 Beyond Jon Snow, examples of bastards include Ramsey Snow and the Sand Snakes. See Aurelia Desveaux, "Hope for Bastards and Sand Snakes," in *The Ultimate Game of Thrones and Philosophy: You Think or Die*, ed. Eric J. Silverman and Robert Arp (Chicago: Open Court, 2017), 127–32.
6 Evan Rosa, "Jon Snow, a Misshapen Christ Figure," in *Ultimate Game of Thrones and Philosophy*, 54.
7 Beyond the central example of Tyrion, the event which launches the series—Bran being pushed from a window and losing his ability to walk—is also a moment of disability, and Martin's story is filled with disability narratives. Additional examples include Hodor, Varys, Jamie, and Arya. See Pascal J. Massie and Lauryn S. Mayer, "Bringing Elsewhere Home: *A Song of Ice and Fire*'s Ethics of Disability," *Studies in Medievalism* 23 (2014): 45–59; Charles Lambert, "A Tender Spot in My Heart," *Critical Quarterly* 57.1 (2015): 20–33; Colleen Elaine Donnelly, "Revisioning Negative Archetypes of Disability and Deformity in Fantasy: *Wicked*, *Maleficent*, and *Game of Thrones*," *Disability Studies Quarterly* 36.4 (2016), https://dsq-sds.org/article/view/5313; Jeremy Pierce, "Bran, Hodor, and Disability in Westeros," in *Ultimate Game of Thrones and Philosophy*, 101–8; and Kimberly S. Engels, "Guilty of Being a Dwarf," in *Ultimate Game of Thrones and Philosophy*, 37–43. While many of Martin's representations of disability are progressive, that judgment is qualified by them being almost all male, as argued by Courtney Stanton, "Learn to Fight with Your Other Hand: *Game of Thrones* as a Complicated Champion of Disability," in *Fan Phenomena: Game of Thrones*, ed. Kavita Mudan Finn (Bristol: Intellect, 2017), 140–50.

8 See *Richard III* (2004), dir. Peter DuBois, at the Public Theatre (New York).
9 See Jaime Hovey, "Tyrion's Gallantry," *Critical Quarterly* 57.1 (2015): 86–98.
10 Rikke Schubart, "Woman with Dragons: Daenerys, Pride, and Postfeminist Possibilities," in *Women of Ice and Fire: Gender Game of Thrones, and Multiple Media Engagements*, ed. Anne Gjelsvik and Rikke Schubart (London: Bloomsbury, 2016), 113.

14 Girl power
Mimetic feminism and rhetorical misogyny

Along with the proliferation of the stigmatized protagonist, the representation of strong female characters is the best evidence for the case that George R.R. Martin was influenced by Shakespeare's first tetralogy as a literary work rather than just the Wars of the Roses as a historical event.[1] But the shared tropes for female characters also point to one of the biggest differences between these two texts: the way each author engaged with the gender politics of his time.

In medieval England, to quote Eileen Power, "the Church and aristocracy combined to establish the doctrine of the woman's subjugation."[2] Women were expected to be submissive to their husbands and remain within the domestic realm of home-making and child-rearing. Among others, Queen Elizabeth I disrupted that gender ideology, showing that a woman could be a successful sovereign and didn't need a husband.[3]

What is the relationship between the long, prosperous, and fairly stable reign of Elizabeth I and the women in Shakespeare's *Henry VI*—Joan, Margaret, and Eleanor—who are warriors, governors, and ambitious for power?[4] Why are all three accused of witchcraft? And how do the witchy women of Shakespeare's first tetralogy relate to the warrior women, dragon queens, and witches in *Game of Thrones*?

Coding political women as witches was an expression of male anxiety about the increased power and prominence of women in the Elizabethan age.[5] Their power, the trope suggested, couldn't come from themselves; it had to come from some external, supernatural, and illicit source. Thus in *1 Henry VI*, Joan of Arc, while a "shepherd's daughter" (1.3.51)—associating her with the pastoral mode and its focus on domestic affairs—pulls from religious symbols to announce her arrival as a military leader:

> Heaven and our Lady gracious hath it pleased
> To shine on my contemptible estate....

God's mother deignèd to appear to me,
And, in a vision full of majesty,
Willed me to leave my base vocatïon,
And free my country from calamity.

(1.3.53–60)

Shakespeare and his collaborators presented the woman warrior as supernatural because a domestic life for women was thought to be natural, Joan coordinating her military prowess with her rejection of traditional femininity.[6] "My courage try by combat, if thou dar'st," she challenges Charles, the French Dauphin, "And thou shalt find that I exceed my sex" (1.3.68–69). Because Joan's emergence as a strong female character threatens traditional gender ideology, the Dauphin tries to contain her exceptionality by reading traditional feminine qualities—namely, beauty—into her military prowess and sexualizing her: "Impatiently I burn with thy desire. / My heart and hands thou hast at once subdued" (1.3.87–88). One of the obstacles of being a political woman in a patriarchal world is dealing with men who can only conceive of you as a sexual object, as repeatedly occurs in *Game of Thrones*.

Where the French read Joan's military might as divine intervention, the opposing English see it as a sign of the demonic: "A woman clad in armour chaseth men. / Devil, or devil's dam, I'll conjure thee. / Blood will I draw on thee—thou art a witch" (1.7.3–6). Like the English characters in the text, the English authors of the text saw Joan as a witch, going as far as to stage actual supernatural visitors for her: "Now, ye familiar spirits that are culled / Out of the powerful regions under earth, / Help me this once, that France may get the field" (5.4.10–12). The French reading of Joan's divinity and the English reading of her demonism are similar in that they refuse to allow a woman's physical and political strength to be earthly and natural. The difference between the French reading of Joan as a messenger of God and the English reading of her as a servant of the devil is that the English reading authorizes cruelty and violence against her, as when the Duke of York spurns her as a "strumpet" (5.7.84) while sentencing her to be burned at the stake: "Curse, miscreant, when thou comest to the stake" (5.5.15); "Bring forth that sorceress condemned to burn" (5.7.1). Four hundred years later, the motif of the burning girl would become central to *Game of Thrones*, not only in Daenerys's self-immolation, which radically revises the trope, but also in the sacrifice of Shireen, which devastatingly retains it.[7]

In the same scene that Joan is sentenced to burn at the stake, the second major female character in Shakespeare's first tetralogy appears for the first time, Joan's French countrywoman Margaret of Anjou. Margaret does not start out with any supernatural coding because she begins as an objectified, sexualized woman contained within the gender ideology of patriarchy: "She's beautiful, and therefore to be wooed; / She is a woman, therefore to be won" (*1 Henry VI*, 5.6.34–35). The biggest difference between Joan and Margaret is that the latter does enter into romantic relationships. First, Margaret is treated like chattel in a patriarchal system where fathers hand women off to husbands: "I perceive I am thy prisoner," she says to King Henry's suitor (1.5.6.30). After being married off without any say in the matter, Margaret, echoing Joan, starts to develop skills in a field traditionally dominated by men. Before becoming a warrior like Joan, Margaret becomes a politician. In this realm, Margaret must, like Joan, field sexist comments from the patriarchy—"These are no women's matters," the Duke of Gloucester tells her (*2 Henry VI*, 1.3.116)—but Margaret, again like Joan, affirms her ability to play the men's game: "Am I a queen in title and in style, / And must be made a subject to a duke?" (*2 Henry VI*, 1.3.47–48). After King Henry disinherits their son by naming the Duke of York heir to the throne (1.1.174–75), Margaret becomes the political power broker in their marriage (e.g., 1.3.113–20). For romance, she turns to the Duke of Suffolk but, when he is banished (3.3.343–52), all of her attention focuses on her son, the prince. Her fierce protection of her son and his right to rule becomes Margaret's definitive characteristic. That specifically feminine trope manifests, however, in the imagery of masculinity when Margaret becomes a Joan and dons armor to lead the military campaign to take back her son's birth right: women are "soft, mild, pitiful, and flexible," the Duke of York says, while she is "stern, obdurate, flinty, rough, remorseless" (*3 Henry VI*, 1.4.141–42). In response, Margaret orders York's head to be cut off and put on a pike (*3 Henry VI*, 1.4.179). Later, the son that Margaret loves so much is murdered right in front of her eyes (*3 Henry VI*, 5.5.38) and, like Joan, Margaret is called an "foul wrinkled witch" and subjected to scorn once she is captured by opposing forces (*Richard III*, 1.3.162).

A third female character, Eleanor, Duchess of Gloucester, solidifies the pattern: an ambitious woman associated with witchcraft has her pursuit of power curtailed. As Kavita Mudan Finn has shown, Shakespeare was the first to intertwine the stories of Margaret and Eleanor.[8] Like Margaret, Eleanor is ambitious and schooled in Machiavellian scheming and backstabbing (she dreams of Gloucester becoming king and herself queen [*2 Henry VI*, 1.2.1–31]). Like Joan, Eleanor conjures up a demonic fiend to aid her pursuit of power (1.4.1–38). The witch Eleanor recruited is burned at the stake (2.3.7) but, because she is noble-born, Eleanor is punished with "three days open penance" (2.3.11) where she is

> Mailed up in shame, with papers on my back,
> And followed with a rabble that rejoice
> To see my tears, and hear my deep-fet groans.
> The ruthless flint doth cut my tender feet,
> And when I start, the envious people laugh
> And bid me be advisèd how I tread.
>
> (2.4.32–37)

It seems likely that Martin had Eleanor's public shaming in mind when he conceived Cersei's walk of atonement (5.10).

From Shakespeare's three main female characters—Joan, Margaret, and Eleanor—we can distill three main character types that inform the two central female characters in *Game of Thrones*: the woman warrior, the momma bear, and the Machiavellian lady.[9] Daenerys is a Margaret (married off against her will) who becomes a Joan (woman warrior), while Cersei is a mixture of Margaret (queen mother) and Eleanor (Machiavellian lady). Cersei never becomes a warrior woman, but she does say to her husband, "I should wear the armor, and you the gown" (1.6), an echo of both Margaret telling Henry VI, "I am ready to put armour on" (*3 Henry VI*, 4.1.103), and Richard III telling her, "You might still have worn the petticoat, / And ne'er have stol'n the breech from Lancaster" (*3 Henry VI*, 5.5.23–24). In some places, the parallels are shockingly pristine, as in Cersei and Margaret's fierce love for their princely sons, and Cersei and Eleanor's public penance. In other places, the parallels are meaningfully transformed: Joan is burned alive as a witch on a pyre, while Daenerys flips this script by burning the witch Mirri Maz Duur and then herself emerging alive from a burned pyre. When she does, Daenerys's dragons become the structural parallel to Joan's fiends, each a supernatural aid in the warrior woman's military plight. But where Joan's fiends forsake her, Daenerys's dragons embrace and empower her. As Karen Gresham illustrates, Daenerys's empowerment is symbolized in "her monstrous and grotesque emotional and physical transformations," like Joan ("witch," "miscreant") and Margaret ("foul wrinkled witch").[10]

These Shakespearean female tropes also extend to other women in *Game of Thrones*. Arya is clearly a Joan: her narrative is centered upon her preference for military over domestic matters and the concomitant inversion of traditional gender roles, leading her to be a woman in armor often coded with masculine regalia.[11] Yara/Asha Greyjoy and

Brienne of Tarth are also Joans: Brienne's name seems to be deliberately modeled on Joan's, as does the image of an armored woman on horseback carrying her banner.[12] Like Cersei, Sansa is a Margaret: though she never dons armor, Sansa is treated as chattel and married off (repeatedly) without much say in the matter, sorely disappointed by her husband's weakness, and disillusioned with romantic love, leading her to turn to a life of politics and to become a powerbroker in her own right.[13] Sansa's mother, Catelyn Stark, also has shades of Margaret: a partner in a political marriage, a momma bear protector of her princely son, and an accidental general in a civil war. Margery Tyrell is the Machiavellian lady of Margaret and Eleanor. Melisandre is an Eleanor. Powerful women coded as witches fill *Game of Thrones*.[14]

There is perhaps no greater debate about *Game of Thrones* than its representation of women, especially because the show presents "unspeakable acts of (sexual) terror," as Anne Gjelsvik writes, "as quality television."[15] Those debates, like Martin's characters, have Shakespearean ancestors, as discussed in the next section. For now, I'll conclude by observing that, while Shakespeare's first tetralogy and *Game of Thrones* have some remarkably similar female characters, the radically different contexts in which those characters were created reveals important differences between Shakespeare and Martin's artistic approaches to the question of women in power. Specifically, in keeping with the genre of history, Shakespeare's approach to women was *mimetic*, his strong female characters reflecting the increased power and stature of women in the age of Elizabeth. Given the survival of these strong female characters in *Game of Thrones*, and Martin's plainly professed feminism, what are we to make of all the retrograde approaches to gender in the show—the sexploitation, the constant misogyny, and the frequent use of rape as a plot point?[16] Working in the fantasy genre, Martin's representation of women was not mimetic but *rhetorical*: rather than reflect the reality of the achievements of modern feminism and women's increased status in the twenty-first century, Martin threw his audience back into a pre-modern world that spotlighted the lingering problems of sexism today. Martin's goal was not to celebrate or even register the achievements of feminism; instead, he sought to advance the feminist cause even further through an authorial bait-and-switch. By first luring his audience into a primitive male fantasy full of sexual conquest and dominance, and then pulling back the curtain on the pain and suffering caused by patriarchy, and revealing women to be the most capable political leaders, Martin and his co-creators secured the investment of the audience they were hoping to enlighten. That strategy has clear liabilities for female and feminist audiences, as registered, for example, in the fan fiction rewriting Sansa's story without rape, which Janice Liedl discusses.[17] But, whether fantasy literature fans or HBO bros, the male audiences drawn to *Game of Thrones* were not initially predisposed to an openness to feminist politics. They came for the dragons and nudity and, once those carnal desires were met, the authors switched from giving audiences what they wanted to giving them what they needed.

Notes

1 The question of Martin's strong female characters is taken up, and debated, by Valerie Estelle Frankel, *Women in Game of Thrones* (Jefferson: McFarland, 2014); *Women of Ice and Fire: Gender Game of Thrones, and Multiple Media Engagements*, ed. Anne Gjelsvik and Rikke Schubart (London: Bloomsbury, 2016); *Game of Thrones Versus History: Written in Blood*, ed. Brian Pavlac (Hoboken: Wiley Blackwell, 2017), esp. Kavita Mudan Finn, "High and Mighty Queens of Westeros" (19–32), and Nicole M. Mares, "Writing the Rules of Their Own Game: Medieval Female Agency and *Game of Thrones*" (147–60); and *Queenship and the Women of Westeros: Female Agency and Advice in Game of Thrones and A Song of Ice and Fire*, ed. Lisa Benz and Zita Eva Rohr (New York: Palgrave Macmillan, 2019), esp. Sylwia Borowska-Szerszun, "Westerosi Queens: Medievalist Portrayal of Female Power and Authority in *A Song of Ice and Fire*" (53–76). See also Section XV below.
2 Eileen Power, *Medieval Women* (London: Cambridge University Press, 1975), 11.
3 See Carole Levin, *The Heart and Stomach of a King: Elizabeth I and the Politics of Sex and Power*, second ed. (Philadelphia: University of Pennsylvania Press, 2013).
4 The connection between Elizabeth and the women in Shakespeare's first tetralogy is explored by Leah Marcus, "Elizabeth," in *Puzzling Shakespeare: Local Reading and Its Discontents* (Berkeley: University of California Press, 1988), 51–105; Nina S. Levine, *Women's Matters: Politics, Gender, and Nation in Shakespeare's Early History Plays* (Newark: University of Delaware Press, 1998); and Swati Ganguli, "Monarchy and Misogyny: Queen Elizabeth I and the Representation of Joan in *1 Henry VI*," *Journal of Drama Studies* 4.2 (2010): 67–76.
5 See Kristin M. Smith, "Martial Maids and Murdering Mothers: Women, Witchcraft and Motherly Transgression in *Henry VI* and *Richard III*," *Shakespeare* 3.2 (2007): 143–60; Nathalie Rivère de Carles, "Acceptable Amazons? Female Warriors on the English and French Early Modern Stage," *Anglophonia* 27 (2010): 203–17.
6 See Danielle Woolley, "Negating Female Power: The Supernatural 'Woman'," *Shakespeare Institute Review* 2 (2013): 23–29.
7 See Rachel M.E. Wolfe, "The 'Most Shocking' Death: Adaptation, Femininity and Victimhood in the Human Sacrifice of Shireen Baratheon," in *Vying for the Iron Throne: Essays on Power, Gender, Death and Performance in HBO's Game of Thrones*, ed. Lindsey Mantoan, Sara Brady (Jefferson: McFarland, 2018), 95–108.

8 Kavita Mudan Finn, "Tragedy, Transgression, and Women's Voices: The Cases of Eleanor Cobham and Margaret of Anjou," *Viator* 47.2 (2016): 277–304.
9 On the woman warrior, see Ken Mondschein, "Women Warriors of Westeros," in *Game of Thrones and the Medieval Art of War* (Jefferson: McFarland, 2017), 148–73. On the momma bear, see Yvonne Tasker and Lindsay Steenberg, "Women Warriors from Chivalry to Vengeance," in *Women of Fire and Ice*, 171–92. On the Machiavellian lady, see Elizabeth Beaton, "Female Machiavellians in Westeros," in *Women of Ice and Fire*, 193–218.
10 Karin Gresham, "Cursed Womb, Bulging Thighs and Bald Scalp: George R.R. Martin's Grotesque Queen," in *Mastering the Game of Thrones: Essays on George R.R. Martin's A Song of Ice and Fire*, ed. Jes Battis and Susan Johnston (Jefferson: McFarland, 2015), 152.
11 See E.M. Dadlez, "Arya Stark as a Rough Hero," in *The Ultimate Game of Thrones and Philosophy: You Think or Die*, ed. Eric J. Silverman and Robert Arp (Chicago: Open Court, 2017), 3–10.
12 See Catherine Pugh, "Harder and Stronger: Yara Greyjoy and the Ironborn," in *Vying for the Iron Throne*, 79–89; Paul Giladi, "Brienne and the Struggle for Recognition," in *Ultimate Game of Thrones and Philosophy*, 61–67.
13 See Danielle Alesi, "The Power of Sansa Stark: A Representation of Female Agency in Late Medieval England," in *Game of Thrones Versus History*, 161–70.
14 See Mikayla Hunter, "'All Men Must Die, but We Are Not Men': Eastern Faith and Feminine Power in *A Song of Ice and Fire* and HBO's *Game of Thrones*" (145–68), and Sheilagh Ilona O'Brien, "Wicked Women and the Iron Throne: The Twofold Tragedy of Witches as Advisors in Game of Thrones" (205–30), in *Queenship and the Women of Westeros*.
15 Anne Gjelsvik, "Unspeakable Acts of (Sexual) Terror as/in Quality Television," in *Women of Ice and Fire*, 57–78. See also Lori J. Underwood, "Sex, Consent, and Rape in Westeros," in *Ultimate Game of Thrones and Philosophy*, 133–39.
16 See Jessica Salter, "*Game of Thrones*'s George RR Martin: 'I'm a feminist at heart'," *The Telegraph* (April 1, 2013), https://www.telegraph.co.uk/women/womens-life/9959063/Game-of-Throness-George-RR-Martin-Im-a-feminist.html.
17 Janice Liedl, "Unbowed, Unbent, Unaccepted: Disputing Women's Roles in *Game of Thrones*," in *Fan Phenomena: Game of Thrones*, ed. Kavita Mudan Finn (Bristol: Intellect, 2017), 128–39.

15 Generic bias
Gender, race, criticism

Critics usually trace the race and gender problems in *Game of Thrones* to tropes of orientalism and androcentrism in fantasy literature[1]; then to Martin's misguided medievalism holding that the Middle Ages were an all-white hellhole for women[2]; then to choices by showrunners David Benioff and D.B. Weiss that aggravate problems and erase nuance in Martin's books[3]; then to the ongoing structural inequalities in America that both prompt these behaviors and minimize the issues when raised.[4] These forces worked upon Martin and his collaborators as they shaped the Wars of the Roses into *A Song of Ice and Fire*, then *Game of Thrones*. A Shakespearean context reveals, however, that the race and gender problems of *Game of Thrones* are intrinsic to the narrative's source material. *Game of Thrones* inherited the problematic identity politics of Shakespeare's first tetralogy, resulting in parallel critical conversations about racism and sexism in these texts. Operating on the level of narrative structure, these regressive identity politics override progressive moves made by the authors, which are more evident with gender than race, and which come on the lower level of characterization. This dynamic shows how the ethical impulses of individual authors can be stifled by what I term "generic bias," and how generic bias perpetuates harmful attitudes over time.

The Middle Ages were multi-cultural.[5] Medieval England was also patriarchal, especially at the level of nobility. Thus, the story of English royalty was told in Tudor history with no effort to capture the diversity of medieval society; it was told as a story of patrilinear male succession. Unavoidably, the Tudor myth is androcentric and ethnocentric. The national story (of internal feuds among noble English families) was the hub of androcentrism, the international story (of external war with France and Ireland) of ethnocentrism. Conservative identity politics were built into the narrative structure and political purpose of the Tudor myth.

Generic bias: gender, race, criticism 93

Shakespeare, Marlowe, and their co-authors negotiated these identity politics with mixed results. The first tetralogy includes many sexist men and moments—Talbot demeaning Joan (*1 Henry VI*, 1.7), the Duke of York attacking Margaret (*3 Henry VI*, 1.4), Edward IV's creepy wooing of Elizabeth Woodville (*3 Henry VI*, 3.2), Richard III's creepy wooing of Anne (*Richard III*, 1.2), Richard III's creepy wooing of Elizabeth of York (*Richard III*, 4.4)—where readers can debate how much a given character's misogyny reflects the author's.[6] Less debatable is the sexism of the stereotypes Shakespeare and co-authors used to characterize women—Joan, Eleanor, Margaret, and Marjory Jordan as witches; Margaret, Lady Bona, and Elizabeth of York as chattel; Joan and Margaret as masculine; Joan as a whore—and the sexist use of femininity as a metaphor for deficiency (Henry VI as effeminate, France as effeminate, tears as effeminate).[7] At the same time, several female characters avoid stereotypes and become complex and agential, significantly shaping the arc of the narrative, whether as individuals (Joan, Eleanor, and Margaret in *Henry VI*[8]) or as a collective (the choral voice of Margaret, Elizabeth, Anne and the Duchess in *Richard III*[9]). Add to these strong female characters Shakespeare's representation of masculinity and patriarchy as sources of chaos and tragedy—what Jean Howard calls the "spectacular failures of the male-dominated social order" in Shakespeare's first tetralogy—and a more nuanced image of Shakespeare's approach to gender emerges.[10] Arching over these progressive impulses, however, the structure of Shakespeare's first tetralogy remains fundamentally androcentric, moving from one English king to another—Henry V, Henry VI, Edward IV, Edward V, Richard III, Henry VII—while several of the significant women in this story, such as Elizabeth of York, never appear on stage.[11] That generic bias toward men in English history is why Phyllis Rackin called the women in the first tetralogy "anti-historians," Kay Stanton similarly calling Joan "a champion of the 'anti-historical' voice."[12] In that role, the women of the first tetralogy can be read, along with Kathryn Schwarz, as "invested with female agency even as they are mobilized in the apparent service of normative social imperatives."[13] That is why Manuela S. Rossini sees female heroism as an impossibility in the first tetralogy.[14]

Some of Shakespeare's most misogynistic characters are also his most ethnocentric characters—the Talbot who is "the scourge of France" (*1 Henry VI*, 2.3.14), the Duke of York who fights "the uncivil kerns of Ireland" (*2 Henry VI*, 3.1.310), the Richard III who slanders the "scum of Bretons" (*Richard III*, 5.3.46).[15] As with sexism, nationalism often ascends from the level of character's words to that of author's characterizations: the French speak in silly stage accents, while the femininity, nationality, and diabolism of their avatar, Joan, are degrading metaphors for each other.[16] Yet real power resides in strong French characters—Joan defeats Talbot (*1 Henry VI*, 1.7), Margaret overpowers the Duke of York (*3 Henry VI*, 1.4)—complicating Shakespeare's ethnocentrism as it does his androcentrism. Two points further nuance the notion of a happily nationalistic Shakespeare: first, as Nina S. Levine writes, "the most serious threat to Talbot—and to England—comes not from the outside, not from low-born French women like Joan, but from within the ranks of the English aristocracy itself"[17]; and second, in Richard Hillman's words, "for the English of the period, France was always, in some measure, their own alienated heritage."[18] Such critics tend to think, along with Ellen C. Caldwell, that the first tetralogy "questions the practice of using foreign war to promote the interests of the state."[19] Yet, just as there is an overarching androcentrism, so too the structural ethnocentrism of the first tetralogy—its centering of English Henries, Edwards, and Richards, and its positioning of other nations as ancillary concerns—curtails both Shakespeare's skepticism of nationalism and his gestures toward cosmopolitanism. While the French get lots of stage time in *1 Henry VI*, the Irish that the Duke of York goes to war against in *2 Henry VI* never appear, an ethnic erasure recalling the gendered erasure of Elizabeth of York.[20]

Given these complexities, when looking at gender in Shakespeare's first tetralogy, some emphasize "the presence and prominence of female characters," others that "Renaissance historiography constituted a masculine tradition, written by men, devoted to the deeds of men, glorifying the masculine virtues of courage, honor, and patriotism, and dedicated to preserving the names of past heroes and recording their patriarchal genealogies."[21] And looking at ethnicity, some argue that Shakespeare and his co-authors in the first tetralogy "cast serious doubt on the Tudor view of history," while others say "we might think of one of the central functions of the history play as rehearsing mythic pasts to support national, racial, and gendered hierarchies."[22]

In sum, the diversity of identities involved in the story of the Wars of the Roses was minimized by the Tudor historians who centered the English men in their royal history. Working with those histories, Shakespeare and his co-authors variously amplified and erased female and foreign voices while perpetuating the centrality of English men in this story. As a result, critical conversations on the identity politics of the first tetralogy show sharp disagreements, with a general sense of longing, given glimpses of progressive identity politics from

Shakespeare and his co-authors, for something more. Ultimately, the conservative generic conventions of the English history play exerted more influence upon the identity politics of the first tetralogy than the progressive innovations Shakespeare, Marlowe, and their co-authors attempted.

Game of Thrones inherited the generic bias of the English history plays from Shakespeare's first tetralogy, and the debates about identity politics in the series are, in part, a function of that inheritance. With respect to gender, *Game of Thrones* has its misogynistic characters—Khal Drogo, Tyrion, Joffrey, Ramsay Bolton, Gregor Clegane, Craster (the list could go on ... very long)—and, more significantly, its misogynistic characterizations. It also has strong female characters and sharp critiques of masculinity and patriarchy. Yet, recalling Shakespeare's first tetralogy, those progressive gestures are subordinated to the structural androcentrism of the story of Westeros moving from Robert Baratheon and Eddard Stark to Brandon Stark and Tyrion Lannister. Given these contrary treatments of gender, some conclude that "Martin's women tend toward the stereotypical," others that "women such as Daenerys Targaryen, Cersei Lannister, Olenna and Margery Tyrell, and Sansa and Arya Stark exhibit independent agency, propelling the storylines."[23] Feminist criticism of Shakespeare's first tetralogy and *Game of Thrones* display parallel debates because the later text derives, in part, from the earlier. The ambivalence in feminist criticism of *Game of Thrones* is not only a function of the variety in the text's representation of women, which is misogynist and feminist at turns, but also a function of the text's indebtedness to Shakespeare's first tetralogy, which is the same.

Similarly, with respect to ethnicity, *Game of Thrones* presents racist characters—"I don't take orders from savages or their sluts" (1.4), "Why are you wasting a woman like this on a Dornishman?" (4.1), "an army of savages ... mindless Unsullied soldiers who will destroy your castles and your holdfasts, Dothraki heathens who will burn your villages to the ground, rape and enslave your women, and butcher your children without a second thought" (7.2)—and racist characterizations: Essos as a second-class continent (ancillary to the centrality of Westeros in the title sequence, for example), Daenerys's white savior narrative (symbolized in the shot of her surrounded by the adoring freed slaves of Yunkai [3.10]), the Spanish Xanadu of the Water Palace in Dorne, the racialized hypersexuality of the Summer Isles ("I will fuck this blond queen," the pirate Salladhor Saan pledges [2.2]), the "brindle-skinned half-men from the jungles of Sothoryos" (*DwD* 758), Martin's Africa. The narrative also includes strong foreign characters—Khal Drogo,

Missandei, Grey Worm—as well as a critique of Westerosi nationalism, imperialism, and colonialism. The Mereneese knot subverts Daenerys's white savior narrative, and the narrative draws attention to the waves of colonizers—the First Men, the Andals, the Targaryens—who settled Westeros, displacing the indigenous Children of the Forest. Those gestures come in the context of the structural ethnocentrism of a story that centers upon three white Westerosi characters—Jon, Daenerys, and Tyrion—and that, in the books, has no point-of-view chapters from people of color until Arianne Martell in the fourth book, a character then cut from the show. The story of Jalabhar Xho, an exile from the Summer Islands, is never told in *A Song of Ice and Fire* (it is relegated to *The World of Ice & Fire*). As Shiloh Carroll writes, "Martin is content to portray the eastern cultures and characters entirely externally, with no attempt to explain their behavior or traditions from the inside."[24] The show furthermore turns Xaro Xhoan Daxos into "a savage from the Summer Isles" (2.4); turns the multi-ethnic slaves in Slaver's Bay into largely people of color; presents hordes of brown people in armies—the Dothraki, the Unsullied—with few individuated characters; somehow simultaneously whitewashes and exoticizes the Sand Snakes; blithely sends the Dothraki to their deaths *en masse*; and kills off its only woman of color with a speaking role, Missandei, to set up the story of a white protagonist.

The identity politics of the first tetralogy and *Game of Thrones* are not a simple case of textual ambiguity leading to critical ambivalence on the order of the *Duck/Rabbit* that Norman Rabkin associated with Shakespeare's history plays.[25] Rather, there are retrograde ideologies of gender and ethnicity codified on the level of genre curtailing progressive flashes on the lower level of character, leading to disputes arising from critics emphasizing one level or the other.

Theorizing outward, *generic bias* is the notion that literary traditions can include structural inequalities codified through repetition over time that result in retrograde representations of identity, which may be unbeknownst to authors or even contrary to their purposeful designs. The generic bias toward English royalty in history plays led Shakespeare to exclude women and include both ethnocentric depictions of other nations and classist representations of working people. These gender, ethnic, and class biases in Shakespeare informed the genre of historical fiction that influenced Martin, while *Game of Thrones* added the generic biases of fantasy literature, specifically the orientalizing depictions of race. On the one hand, the generic biases of historical fiction help us understand why Martin centers whiteness and maleness, excluding women, black, and brown characters from leading roles and in-depth development. On the other hand, the generic biases of fantasy help us understand why Martin included racist stereotypes in cases where he does include black and brown characters. Considering generic bias beyond fantasy, we can speak, for example, of the classism of tragedy, the anti-semitism of the conversion narrative, the ageism of the bildungsroman, the heteronormativity of the romantic comedy, and the ableism of the superhero story. In each case, generic bias excludes certain identities from representation, uses offensive stereotypes for those included, and perpetuates these conventions over time—often quite apart from any deliberate authorial intent, sometimes in tension with egalitarian authorial efforts. With generic bias, retrograde conventions of narrative structure often outweigh progressive innovations on the lower level of characterization. The result is that criticism oriented toward social justice displays an ambivalence toward texts that may captivate audiences in many ways yet retain the superstructures of generic bias. Generic bias then offers up a ready-made (if feeble) defense—*That's just how things are done in this genre*—when problematic representations of identity are identified and critiqued.

Notes

1 See Helen Young, "The Real Middle Ages: Dirty Fantasy," in *Race and Popular Fantasy Literature: Habits of Whiteness* (New York: Routledge, 2016), 63–87; Mat Hardy, "The Crack of Dorne," in *Vying for the Iron Throne: Essays on Power, Gender, Death and Performance in HBO's Game of Thrones*, ed. Lindsey Mantoan, Sara Brady (Jefferson: McFarland, 2018), 16–27; Mat Hardy, "The East Is Least: The Stereotypical Imagining of Essos in *Game of Thrones*," *Canadian Review of American Studies* 49.1 (2019): 26–45.

2 See Kathleen E. Kennedy, "'Game of Thrones' Is Even Whiter Than You Think," *Vice* (Oct. 18 2016), https://www.vice.com/en_us/article/8gexwp/game-of-thrones-is-even-whiter-than-you-think; Helen Young, "Game of Thrones' Racism Problem," *The Public Medievalist* (July 21, 2017), https://www.publicmedievalist.com/game-thrones-racism-problem/; Shiloh Carroll, "Race in A Song of Ice and Fire: Medievalism Posing as Authenticity," *The Public Medievalist* (Nov. 28, 2017), https://www.publicmedievalist.com/race-in-asoif/; Kavita Mudan Finn, "Decolonizing Popular Medievalism: The Case of *Game of Thrones*" (March 28, 2018), https://kvmfinn.wordpress.com/2018/03/28/decolonizing-popular-medievalism-the-case-of-game-of-thrones/; Kavita Mudan Finn, "*Game of Thrones* is Based in History—Outdated History," *The Public Medievalist* (May 16, 2019), https://www.publicmedievalist.com/thrones-outdated-history/.

3 See Shiloh Carroll, "Tone Deaf?: *Game of Thrones*, Showrunners and Criticism," in *HBO's Original Voices: Race, Gender, Sexuality and Power*, ed. Victoria McCollum and Giuliana Monteverde (New York: Routledge,

98 *Generic bias: gender, race, criticism*

  2018), 169–82; Kavita Mudan Finn, "Queen of Sad Mischance: Medievalism, 'Realism,' and the Case of Cersei Lannister," in *Queenship and the Women of Westeros: Female Agency and Advice in Game of Thrones and A Song of Ice and Fire*, ed. Lisa Benz and Zita Eva Rohr (New York: Palgrave Macmillan, 2019), 29–52.
4 See Saladin Ahmed, "Is 'Game of Thrones' Too White?," *Salon* (April 1, 2012), https://www.salon.com/2012/04/01/is_game_of_thrones_too_white/; Mat Hardy, "The Eastern Question," in *Game of Thrones versus History: Written in Blood*, ed. Brian Pavlac (Hoboken: Wiley Blackwell, 2017), 97–110; Mat Hardy, "Godless Savages and Lockstep Legions: Examining Military Orientalism in *Game of Thrones*," *Journal of Asia-Pacific Pop Culture* 4.2 (2019): 192–212; Roberta Garrett, "'A Sly and Stubborn People': *Game of Thrones*, Orientalism and Islamophobia," in *Contesting Islamophobia: Anti-Muslim Prejudice in Media, Culture and Politics*, ed. Peter Morey, Amina Yaqin, and Alaya Forte (London: Bloomsbury, 2019), 103–22.
5 See the series *Race, Racism, and the Middle Ages*, in *The Public Medievalist*, ed. Paul B. Sturtevant (2017-Press), https://www.publicmedievalist.com/race-racism-middle-ages-toc/; Yvonne Seale, "The Multi-Cultural Middle Ages: An Annotated Bibliography for Teachers," in *The Once and Future Classroom: Resources for Teaching the Middle Ages* 14.1 (Fall 2017), https://once-and-future-classroom.org/the-multicultural-middle-ages-an-annotated-bibliography-for-teachers-of-middle-and-high-school-students/.
6 See, for example, Ian Frederick Moulton, "'A Monster Great Deformed': The Unruly Masculinity of Richard III," *Shakespeare Quarterly* 47 (1996): 251–68; Romuald Ian Lakowski, "From History to Myth: The Misogyny of Richard III in More's *History* and Shakespeare's Play," *QWERTY* 9 (1999): 15–23.
7 See Gabriele Bernhard Jackson, "Topical Ideology: Witches, Amazons, and Shakespeare's Joan of Arc," *English Literary Renaissance* 18 (1988): 40–65; Nancy A. Gutierrez, "Gender and Value in *1 Henry VI*: The Role of Joan de Pucelle," *Theatre Journal* 42 (1990): 183–93; James J. Paxson, "Shakespeare's Medieval Devils and Joan la Pucelle in *1 Henry VI*: Semiotics, Iconography, and Feminist Criticism," in *Henry VI: Critical Essays*, ed. Thomas A. Pendleton (New York: Routledge, 2001), 127–55; Miguel Ángel González Campos, "'An Effeminate Prince': Gender Construction in Shakespeare's First Tetralogy," *SEDERI* 12 (2001): 229–35; Albert H. Tricomi, "Joan la Pucelle and the Inverted Saints Play in *1 Henry VI*," *Renaissance and Reformation* 25.2 (2001): 5–31; Martha A. Kurtz, "Tears and Masculinity in the History Play: Shakespeare's Henry VI," in *Grief and Gender: 700–1700*, ed. Jennifer C. Vaught (New York: Palgrave Macmillan, 2003), 163–76; Patrick Ryan, "Shakespeare's Joan and the Great Whore of Babylon," *Renaissance and Reformation* 28.4 (2004): 55–82; Kristin M. Smith, "Martial Maids and Murdering Mothers: Women, Witchcraft, and Motherly Transgression in *Henry VI* and *Richard III*," *Shakespeare* 3 (2007): 143–60; Dorothea Kehler, "Canard and the Common Lot: The Making of Shakespeare's Margaret of Anjou," *Journal of Drama Studies* 1 (2007): 4–19; Tom Mandall, "Mothers, Murder, and Gender Transgression: Queen Margaret in *Henry VI Part 3*," *Birmingham Journal of Literature and Language* 4 (2012): 6–15.

8 See H. Austin Whitver, "Erecting a Pyramid in France: Tomb Symbolism in *1 Henry VI*," *Journal for Early Modern Cultural Studies* 15.3 (2015): 82–101; Nina S. Levine, "The Case of Eleanor Cobham: Authorizing History in *2 Henry VI*," *Shakespeare Studies* 22 (1994): 104–21; Nicole Rowan, "Is There a Woman in This Text? Female Domination in Shakespeare's *Henry VI*," *Links and Letters* 2 (1995): 31–45.
9 See Mario DiGangi, "Competitive Mourning and Female Agency in *Richard III*," in *A Feminist Companion to Shakespeare*, ed. Dympna Callaghan (Oxford: Wiley Blackwell, 2016), 428–39; Cristina León Alfar, "Speaking Truth to Power as Feminist Ethics in *Richard III*," *Social Research* 86.3 (2019): 789–819.
10 Jean E. Howard, "Stage Masculinities, National History, and the Making of London Theatrical Culture," in *Center or Margin: Revisions of the English Renaissance in Honor of Leeds Barroll*, ed. Lena Cowen Orlin (Selinsgrove: Susquehanna University Press, 2006), 199.
11 On the absence of Elizabeth of York, see Kavita Mudan Finn, *The Last Plantagenet Consorts: Gender, Genre, and Historiography, 1440–1627* (New York: Palgrave Macmillan, 2012), 144–72.
12 Phyllis Rackin, "Anti-Historians: Women's Roles in Shakespeare's Histories," *Theatre Journal* 37 (1985): 329–44; Kay Stanton, "A Presentist Analysis of Joan, la Pucelle: 'What's Past and What's to Come She Can Descry'," in *Presentism, Gender, and Sexuality in Shakespeare*, ed. Evelyn Gajowski (New York: Palgrave Macmillan, 2009), 105.
13 Kathryn Schwarz, "A Tragedy of Good Intentions: Maternal Agency in *3 Henry VI* and *King John*," *Renaissance Drama* 32 (2003), 226–27.
14 Manuela S. Rossini, "The Sexual/Textual Impossibility of Female Heroism in the First Tetralogy," *Shakespeare Yearbook* 14 (2004): 45–78.
15 See, for example, Ralph Berry, "Richard III: Bonding the Audience," in *Mirror up to Shakespeare: Essays in Honor of G. R. Hibbard*, ed. J.C. Gray (Toronto: University of Toronto Press, 1984), 114–27.
16 Lisa Hopkins, "French Accents in Shakespeare's *Henry VI* Plays," *Folio: Shakespeare-Genootschap van Nederland en Vlaanderen* 3.1 (1996): 5–10; Bernhard Klein, "'Tale of Iron Wars': Shakespeare and the Uncommon Soldier," in *War and the Cultural Construction of Identities in Britain*, ed. Barbara Korte and Ralf Schneider (Amsterdam: Rodopi, 2002), 93–107; Karma Waltonen, "Saint Joan: From Renaissance Witch to New Woman," *Shaw: The Annual of Bernard Shaw Studies* 24 (2004): 186–203; Amanda Penlington, "'Not a Man from England': Assimilating the Exotic 'Other' through Performance, from *Henry IV* to *Henry VI*," in *This England, That Shakespeare: New Angles on Englishness and the Bard*, ed. Willy Maley and Margaret Tudeau-Clayton (Burlington: Ashgate, 2010), 165–83; and Janet Suzman, "The Two Joans," in *Not Hamlet: Meditations on the Frail Position of Women in Drama* (London: Oberon, 2012): 110–24.
17 Nina S. Levine, *Women's Matters: Politics, Gender, and Nation in Shakespeare's Early History Plays* (Newark: University of Delaware Press, 1998), 27.
18 Richard Hillman, *Shakespeare, Marlowe, and the Politics of France* (New York: Palgrave, 2002), 13.
19 Ellen C. Caldwell, "The Hundred Years' War and National Identity," in *Inscribing the Hundred Years' War in French and English Cultures*, ed. Denise N. Baker (Albany: State University of New York Press, 2000), 259.

100 *Generic bias: gender, race, criticism*

20 On the erasure of the Irish, see Stephen O'Neill, *Staging Ireland: Representations in Shakespeare and Renaissance Drama* (Dublin: Four Courts, 2007).
21 Jean Howard and Phyllis Rackin, *Engendering a Nation: A Feminist Account of Shakespeare's English Histories* (New York: Routledge, 1997), 23; Phyllis Rackin, *Stages of History: Shakespeare's English Chronicles* (Ithaca: Cornell University Press, 1990), 147.
22 David L. Frey, *The First Tetralogy, Shakespeare's Scrutiny of the Tudor Myth: A Dramatic Exploration of Divine Providence* (The Hague: Mouton, 1976), 2; Francesca T. Royster, "The Chicago Shakespeare Theater's Rose Rage: Whiteness, Terror, and the Fleshwork of Theatre in a Post-Colorblind Age," in *Colorblind Shakespeare: New Perspectives on Race and Performance*, ed. Ayanna Thompson (New York: Routledge, 2006), 221.
23 Shiloh R. Carroll, "'You Ought to be in Skirts and Me in Mail': Gender and History in George R.R. Martin's A Song of Ice and Fire," in *George R.R. Martin's 'A Song of Ice and Fire' and the Medieval Literary Tradition*, ed. Bartłomiej Błaszkiewicz (Warsaw: Warsaw University Press, 2014), 258; Zita Eva Rohr and Lisa Benz, Introduction to *Queenship and the Women of Westeros*, xxxvi.
24 Shiloh Carroll, "Postcolonialism, Slavery, and the Great White Hope," in *The Medievalism of A Song of Ice and Fire and Game of Thrones* (Cambridge: DS Brewer, 2018), 127.
25 Norman Rabkin, "Rabbits, Ducks, and Henry V," *Shakespeare Quarterly* 28.3 (1977): 279–96.

16 *The Bloody Hand*
Intertextual metatheater

On January 27, 2013, George R.R. Martin released a chapter titled "Mercy" from *The Winds of Winter*, the long-delayed, still-unfinished sixth book in *A Song of Ice and Fire*.[1] It tells the story of the character Mercy, short for Mercedene—who is really Arya Stark—working in a theater in Braavos, performing in a play called *The Bloody Hand*, and revenge-killing an old foe who shows up in the audience. The different versions of *The Bloody Hand* in Martin's chapter and the HBO show are variously intertextual, metatheatrical, and intertextually metatheatrical—meaning they (1) allude to Shakespeare, (2) reflect upon their own acts of artistic representation, and (3) allude to Shakespeare's reflections on art.

Shakespeare did not invent the play-within-the-play or metatheatrical allusions to actors and audiences within dramatic texts. These were established tropes in early-modern drama.[2] But Shakespeare explored this device in depth, writing five plays-within-plays: the production for Sly in *The Taming of the Shrew*, "The Worthies" in *Love's Labor's Lost*, "Pyramus and Thisby" in *A Midsummer Night's Dream*, "The Mousetrap" in *Hamlet*, and "Ceres and Juno" in *The Tempest*. These metadramas always serve two functions: (1) to comment on the events of the central narrative, and (2) to comment on the nature of dramatic signification. So how does *The Bloody Hand* comment on the central narrative of *A Song of Ice and Fire*? What does the inset play—both Martin's version and HBO's—suggest about how these authors understand their art and their audiences?

In Martin's chapter, *The Bloody Hand* is both Shakespearean and deliberately Not-Shakespearean. It alludes to Shakespeare's texts but, in keeping with Martin's concern with social structures, more extensively draws upon the theatrical culture of early-modern London.[3] Past Braavosi play titles sound like early-modern English plays: *The Merchant's Melancholy Daughter*, *Wroth of the Dragonlords*, *The Anguish of the Archon*, and *The Merchant's Lusty Lady*. Like early-modern English plays, these are mixtures of tragedy (with rousing heroic speeches like "Here the last Titan yet stands, astride the stony shoulders of his brothers") and comedy ("Mercy preferred the scene where the fat merchant shat on the Sealord's head"). Rival theater troupes (called "mummers") recall competition in London between, for example, Lord Chamberlain's Men and Lord Admiral's Men. The different theaters of Braavos—The Gate, The Dome, and The Blue Lantern—echo venue names from Shakespeare's day, like The Curtain, The Globe, and The Red Bull. In keeping with the chapter's Not-Shakespeareanism, Arya works at The Gate, which is less fashionable than The Dome, the theater name echoing The Globe, the playhouse most associated with Shakespeare. The Gate is in the grittier part of town, "but here between the harbors they would never lack for sailors and whores to fill their pit." The building's architecture resembles early-modern theaters, with shades of football stadiums, including different levels for different classes, private boxes on the second balcony, and cheap seats up top. "You have to please the pit," says Izembaro, "King o' the Mummers," that title evoking the Player King in *Hamlet*. As for the author of *The Bloody Hand*, "Phario Forel had written it, and he had the bloodiest quill of all of Braavos": sounds more like John Webster than Shakespeare.

"Every mummer's troupe had to have a dwarf": it is hinted that Bobono, the comic dwarf at the Gate, is really Tyrion Lannister in disguise. That creates a layered effect, since *The Bloody Hand* is about House Lannister. The play has two kings, "the fat one and the boy," Robert Baratheon and Joffrey. As the "bloody hand [of the king]" referred to in the title, Tyrion plays a fun-house mirror version of himself. Like Martin's Tyrion, Phario Forel's character alludes to Shakespeare's Richard III. Bobono's opening speech, spoken to the audience while alone on stage, recalls the opening of *Richard III*:

> The seven-faced god has cheated me. My noble sire he made of purest gold, and gold he made my siblings, boy and girl. But I am formed of darker stuff, of bones and blood and clay, twisted into this rude shape you see before you.

Shakespeare's Richard III is, in contrast to his hyper-sexual brother Edward, "cheated of feature by dissembling nature," "rudely stamped," and "not shaped for sportive tricks," so he declares in his opening address:

> And therefore, since I cannot prove a lover
> To entertain these fair well-spoken days,

The Bloody Hand: intertextual metatheater   103

I am determinèd to prove a villain,
And hate the idle pleasures of these days.
(*Richard III*, 1.1.14–31)

Phario's Tyrion similarly vows, "As I cannot be the hero, let me be the monster, and lesson them in fear in place of love." Making Tyrion a Richard III is a straightforward allusion in keeping with Martin's earlier use of Shakespeare in *A Song of Ice and Fire*. Martin breaks new ground with *The Bloody Hand*, however, by presenting Arya as a Hamlet whose metatheatrical acting is woven into the acting of revenge.[4] She is assigned to join Izembaro's troupe as part of her training with the Faceless Men. When an envoy from Westeros attends *The Bloody Hand*, Arya recognizes Lord Rafford, and lures him back to her apartment. "She slid her finger down along the inside of his thigh," Martin writes. "When he pressed his hand to his thigh, blood squirted through his fingers." Arya has cut his femoral artery, and the title of the play, *The Bloody Hand*, takes on new meaning. Raff's dying words—"You'll need to carry me"—repeat what Arya's disabled friend, Lommy Greenhands, said just before Raff cruelly murdered him in *A Clash of Kings*.

Like Hamlet, Arya is both devoted to revenge against her enemies and delayed in the performance of it, which Shakespeare and Martin symbolize in the theatrical acting their characters do. Theatrical acting is a metaphor for social acting. Hamlet feigning madness is the corollary to Arya's initiation into the Faceless Men, both characters hiding their true selves. As the plots of their respective texts have lost their forward momentum, and the characters are going in circles, Hamlet and Arya engage in theatrical acting while they are pretending to be someone they're not, trying to figure out who they really are, and unsure about what to do next. This appropriation of *Hamlet* for *The Bloody Hand* is quite different from connecting Tyrion to Richard III. While most Shakespearean allusions in *A Song of Ice and Fire* are to the playwright's characters, plots, and language, *The Bloody Hand* stands out by adopting a Shakespearean strategy of metatheatrical symbolism.

HBO omitted the Shakespearean resonances Martin wrote into *The Bloody Hand*. They replaced Arya's revenge against Raff with revenge against Meryn Trant, but separated the Trant episode (5.10) from the *Bloody Hand* episodes (6.5–6). The play is not called *The Bloody Hand* in the show: there is no corresponding bloody hand in Arya's murder of Raff at the chapter's close. Arya now comes to the theater as a hired assassin charged with killing Lady Crane, one of the actors. These changes remove the frame of revenge from *The Bloody Hand*, erasing the connection to *Hamlet*. Arya's episodes with the actors are still overlain with her experience becoming a faceless person who plays many parts, but the crispness of that conceit is lost because, in the HBO version, Arya is not an actor in the performance but an audience member.

That revision, however, adds new Shakespearean connections to HBO's version of *The Bloody Hand*. First, in a scene cut from the show but included on the bonus features of the DVD, Benioff and Weiss created a metatheatrical satire of controversies in the show's reception.[5] Arya laughs as the play's Robert and Tyrion curse, fart, and slap others around, but an offended audience member purses her lips and rolls her eyes: "Violence and profanity. How original!" The nearby Arya claps back: "Why don't you just leave, then?" *If you don't like it*, Benioff and Weiss were saying to their critics, *you don't have to watch*. The offended audience members stick around until the play's Tyrion rips down Sansa's dress, exposing her breasts. "Utterly gratuitous," says the upset theatergoer. "Disgusting and unacceptable," her friend replies, as they leave.

From a Shakespearean angle, the scene has shades of mocking Polonius's uppity comments when watching "Aeneas's Tale to Dido" in *Hamlet*, which is a different kind of metatheater than "The Mousetrap." One version is actor-oriented, the other audience-oriented. Here the two main concerns of Shakespearean metatheater have been split between our two modern texts: in his chapter, Martin used metatheater to symbolize themes from his central narrative while, on the show, HBO used metatheater to reflect on its own act of representation. Yet the HBO scene feels more like Ben Jonson's metatheater, which often disparages audiences and affirms the author's genius, rather than Shakespeare's, which celebrates the audience's imagination as a key element in the process of artistic signification.[6] "That crowd was shit," HBO's Izembaro says backstage after the play. "These people, worse than animals" (6.6). In its own brand of Not Shakespeareanism, HBO's *The Bloody Hand* envisions an antagonistic, hierarchical relationship between author and audience, like Jonson calling his crowds "base Detractors, and illiterate Apes."[7] In contrast, Shakespearean metatheater tends to take aim at inept and overconfident actors and authors: the most memorable example is Bottom the Weaver. Perhaps Benioff and Weiss cut their satire of offended audience members in an effort not to be the sort of self-righteous authors that Shakespeare often satirized. Cutting that scene also indicates their recognition, in later seasons of *Game of Thrones*, that the show had often missed the mark in its representations of nudity and sexuality. In the wake of cultural conversations about Sansa's rape in Season 5, it would have been

tone-deaf at best for *Game of Thrones* to mock audience members concerned about harmful representations of sexual violence.[8]
According to Jack Bender, who directed the episode,

> David and Dan wrote those scenes somewhat tongue in cheek. Kind of mocking some of the history of the show. And I took it a step farther. I rehearsed it like a play. There's a lot more to that play than ended up in the show. Then I ran the whole show for the show-runners, like we were the *Game of Thrones* Players.[9]

The episode took Bender back to his early theatrical work with Shakespeare. He started out acting in and directing Shakespearean plays, as well as adaptations like *Rosencrantz and Guildenstern are Dead* and *The Tempest*.[10] Deftly drawing upon the comical qualities of Shakespearean metatheater, Bender's *The Bloody Hand* is a farce. The jangly couplets of dialogue recall "The Mousetrap," Bender's faux-antiquated, amateur-hour staging resembling stilted enactments of "The Mousetrap," as in Kenneth Branagh's popular *Hamlet* (1996) film. As with "The Mousetrap," one effect of hyperbolically artificial metadrama is to make the main story, by comparison, seem more realistic. Another is to emphasize the crudeness of the culture represented, making the main text and its audience feel more modern, sophisticated, accomplished. You might not like *Game of Thrones*, the show was saying to audiences, but it's better than *The Bloody Hand*.

By shifting the genre of the playlet from tragedy to farce, HBO's version of *The Bloody Hand* brings audiences to reconsider earlier understandings of the main narrative. The game of thrones that felt so serious in earlier seasons is rendered, through this comic retelling, a ludicrous travesty. The nobility are fools farting, burping, and slapping their way through matters of state. Arya enjoys these parodies when they are aimed at the Lannisters, but becomes unsettled when they contravene her preferred understanding of the past. Her father, Ned Stark, is played as an ambitious clown. His decapitation—though campily staged with a wooden head, to much laughter from the audience—greatly distresses Arya, who saw her father's execution from a crowd similar to the one she finds herself in now. The shift in the tone of the scene mirrors her journey in the show from carefree childhood pleasures to weighty adult responsibilities. That shift culminates when, backstage after the show, Arya advises Lady Crane on rewrites for Cersei's final speech: "She wouldn't just cry. She would be angry. She would want to kill the person who did this to her" (6.6). The theme of revenge returning to the frame of the play, Arya shifts from

106 The Bloody Hand: intertextual metatheater

onlooker to author of her own narrative, after which she retrieves her sword Needle, forsakes the Faceless Men, regains her identity, declares herself "Arya Stark of Winterfell," and resumes her quest for vengeance by returning to Westeros.

Most successfully, *Game of Thrones* invoked Shakespearean themes through its metatheatrical reflection on historiography. HBO's version of *The Bloody Hand* shows history distorted in the representation of it. Robert Baratheon and Ned Stark, obstacles to the Lannisters now in power, are presented as fools. Joffrey, the former Lannister King of Westeros, is a good sovereign. Cersei, the current Queen Regent, is sincere and sympathetic. Tyrion, now at odds with the Lannisters, is the bawdy rogue of Season 1, not the reformed man of Season 6. Played as a cackling villain, he poisons Joffrey, although in truth it was Olenna Tyrell. Pushed to its upmost limit, the HBO version of *The Bloody Hand* is the show's acknowledgment that history—including Shakespeare's—can be written to please the party in power, and *Game of Thrones* is similarly a story told from a situated perspective, which does not reflect an objective recounting of facts.

Notes

1 George R.R. Martin, "Excerpt from *The Winds of Winter*: Mercy," available at http://archive.is/6UYCu.
2 See Robert James Nelson, *Play within a Play: The Dramatist's Conception of his Art* (New Haven: Yale University Press, 1958), and Arthur Brown, "The Play within a Play: An Elizabethan Dramatic Device," *Essays and Studies* 13 (1960): 36–48.
3 See Andrew Gurr, *Playgoing in Shakespeare's London*, third ed. (Cambridge: Cambridge University Press, 2004).
4 See Peter Mercer, *Hamlet and the Acting of Revenge* (Iowa City: University of Iowa Press, 1987).
5 See "Deleted Scenes," on *Game of Thrones: The Complete Sixth Season* (HBO, 2016).
6 See Alvin B. Kernan, "Shakespeare's and Jonson's View of Public Theatre Audiences," in *Jonson and Shakespeare*, ed. Ian Donaldson (Canberra: Humanities Press, 1983), 74–88.
7 Ben Jonson, *Poetaster* (London: R. Bradock for M. Lownes, 1602), Pr.6–9.
8 See Shiloh Carroll, "Tone Deaf?: *Game of Thrones*, Showrunners and Criticism," in *HBO's Original Voices: Race, Gender, Sexuality and Power*, ed. Victoria McCollum and Giuliana Monteverde (New York: Routledge, 2018), 169–82.
9 Vinnie Mancuso, "Mind-Bender: 'Game of Thrones' Director on Original, Brutal Idea for 'Hold the Door'," *Observer* (May 31, 2016), https://observer.com/2016/05/mind-bender-game-of-thrones-director-on-original-brutal-idea-for-hold-the-door/.
10 See Jack Bender (dir.), *Rosencrantz and Guildenstern Are Dead* (LA Free Festival); Jack Bender (dir.), *The Tempest* (NBC, 1998).

17 The Targaryen myth

The Tudor myth presents Henry VII as a heaven-sent soldier whose divinely sanctioned conquest over the demonic Richard III established the Tudor dynasty as divine-right monarchs drawing their authority to govern not from earth but from God. *A Song of Ice and Fire* has its own mythology of a chosen one, but with a very different outcome.[1] Fans love to debate the identity of "the prince that was promised" (*CoK* 48). The specifics of this prophecy about a savior prince need not concern us here apart from the fact that it is said that the prince will be a Targaryen descendent (*DwD* 23), upholding the parallel between Tudors and Targaryens as the house which ultimately comes into power at the end of the narrative. More importantly, *A Song of Ice and Fire* repeatedly calls the legitimacy of prophecies about princes into question. At first, the red witch Melisandre thinks Stannis Baratheon (who is indeed a Targaryen descendant) is the "chosen one" destined to be king (*SoS* 63). She has visions of his victory, promising its immanence no matter how many setbacks he incurs, going as far as to burn his young daughter at the stake in a blood sacrifice to her Lord of Light. That event clearly leads readers to skepticism about the idea of divinely chosen politicians: "If he commands you to burn children, your Lord is evil," as one character says on the HBO show (6.10). When a defeated Stannis is killed in battle, moreover, his status as a "chosen one" is shown to be a sham. For the rest of the show, Melisandre spends her time admitting that "the great victory [she] saw in the flames, all of it was a lie" (6.2), so she is done "whispering in the ears of kings" (7.3), even as she turns her attention to Jon Snow, and then later Daenerys Targaryen.[2]

But Daenerys's authority to govern stems neither from her royal family lineage nor from some divine decree. Instead, Daenerys draws her authority from her demonstrated ability to wield power effectively in the service of a political ideology that appeals to a broad base of people. She is an appealing character precisely because of her efforts, in Christopher Roman's words, "to make politics responsible to ethics."[3] Her attitude toward society and government first surface when, seeing a bit of her own situation in theirs, Daenerys objects to the enslavement and mistreatment of the Lhazareen women who have been conquered by the Dothraki (1.8). Later, her politics are made clear in her extended campaign to abolish slavery in Essos. Daenerys is a progressive liberal with dragons, mythologizing not the divine-right monarchy of the Tudors but a democratic meritocracy. "She's not our queen because she's the daughter of some king we never knew," Missandei says. "She's the queen we chose" (7.4). For his part, Martin has backed Democratic politicians such as Barack Obama, Tom Udall, Hillary Clinton, and Joe Biden.[4] "Politically I'm a liberal Democrat," he said in 2012.[5]

While *Game of Thrones* took from Shakespeare's first tetralogy the notion of a mythological dynasty bringing peace to a land beset by civil war—the Tudors and the Targaryens—the political ideologies represented by Shakespeare's Henry Tudor and Martin's Daenerys Targaryen could not be more different. Where the Tudor myth promoted the idea of a divine-right monarch led by the hand of God to acquire power over a nation, granting that monarch and his descendants absolute authority to rule, the Targaryen myth suggests that political power will seek out, find, and enfranchise those who exercise the most liberal principles, such as freedom, fairness, and equality. While the Tudors and Targaryens mythologize very different political ideologies, Shakespeare and Martin share the literary strategy of propagandizing for the dominant political ideology of the day by ascribing it to their prophesied heroes.

Yet Martin's liberal fantasy is just as much of a myth as divine-right monarchy, and the Targaryen myth is busted in two ways. First, Daenerys's campaign in Slaver's Bay shifts from liberation to occupation. Daenerys variously follows her own will against the advice of loyal council—a symbol of monarchy—and is torn apart by the factional in-fighting Shakespeare associated with children in power, "slowly losing her identity and compromising her principles," as Shiloh Carroll argued.[6] The Targaryen myth was exposed as myth through the fragility of Daenerys's liberalism.

Second, the Targaryen myth was busted in the penultimate episode of the show, where Daenerys turns tyrant, becoming the Mad Queen and burning down King's Landing and many innocent civilians inside. At the same time, the Targaryen myth is reconstituted in the revelation of Jon Snow as the last living Targaryen: the

Night's Watch whence he came is the only true democracy in the show, Priscilla L. Walton argues, "the only instance of a 'one person, one vote' arrangement."⁷

Notes

1 See Michael J. Sigrist, "Fate, Freedom, and Authenticity in *A Game of Thrones*," in *Game of Thrones and Philosophy: Logic Cuts Deeper than Swords*, ed. Henry Jacoby (Hoboken: Wiley, 2012), 223–35; Steph Rennick, "Prophetic Foreknowledge in *Game of Thrones*," in *The Ultimate Game of Thrones and Philosophy: You Think or Die*, ed. Eric J. Silverman and Robert Arp (Chicago: Open Court, 2017), 151–57.
2 For a helpful overview of the religious denominations in the series, see Peter O'Leary, "Sacred Fantasy in *Game of Thrones*," *Critical Quarterly* 57.1 (2015): 6–19. On the religious rhetoric of the War of the Five Kings more generally, see José Luis De Ramón Ruiz, "The Favor of the Gods: Religion and Power in George R. R. Martin's A Song of Ice and Fire," *Fafnir—Nordic Journal of Science Fiction and Fantasy Research* 3.3 (2009): 41–50.
3 Christopher Roman, "The Ethical Movement of Daenerys Targaryen," in *Ethics and Medievalism*, ed. Karl Fugelso (Cambridge: D. S. Brewer; 2014), 61–62.
4 See, for example, Brett Samuels, "Author George RR Martin Backs Biden's candidacy," *The Hill* (May 6, 2019), https://thehill.com/blogs/in-the-know/in-the-know/442280-george-rr-martin-backs-bidens-candidacy.
5 Kathy Wang, "Interview with George R.R. Martin," *Feather Factor* (Feb. 15, 2012), https://www.featherfactor.com/2012/02/interview-with-george-r-r-martin.html.
6 Shiloh Carroll, "Daenerys the Unready: Advice and Ruling in Meereen," in *Queenship and the Women of Westeros: Female Agency and Advice in Game of Thrones and A Song of Ice and Fire*, ed. Lisa Benz and Zita Eva Rohr (New York: Palgrave Macmillan, 2019), 176.
7 Priscilla L. Walton, "'You Win or You Die': The Royal Flush of Power in *Game of Thrones*," *Canadian Review of American Studies* 49.1 (2019), 102.

18 How George R.R. Martin changed the ending of *Game of Thrones*

Spoiler Alert: This section explains details of the author's compositional process. If you hold a Romantic view of literary creation as inspired genius, rather than technical craft, stop reading now.

We know Martin based the structure of his central narrative on the Tudor myth, but was always happy to change things around as needed.[1] My goal here is to show with some specificity how he used character and narrative tropes from Shakespeare's depiction of the Tudor myth as a frame for thinking about several plot developments and possible permutations of his story and its ending. That process can be broken down into five phases.

The first phase is the apparent set-up. When *A Game of Thrones* began with the parallels between Starks-and-Yorks, Lannisters-and-Lancasters, and Targaryens-and-Tudors, this set-up suggested that, after Cersei (as a Margaret of Anjou) killed Eddard Stark (as a Richard, Duke of York), the Stark furthest down in the line of succession, Jon Snow (as a Richard III), who had been stigmatized and barred from power by his bastard birth, and a character audiences find sympathetic and cheer for, would help dethrone the Lannisters and empower the Starks, before then turning against his own family, killing them off, rising through their ranks, and becoming King of Westeros, leaving audiences to wrestle with his transition from protagonist to antagonist—until he was himself unseated by the long-lost claimant to the throne who had been hidden away in a far-off land, Daenerys Targaryen (as a Henry VII), who would then marry one of the Starks (*Hey there, Arya*), unifying the families and ushering in an age of peace and prosperity in Westeros. *What could have been!* Yet that apparent set-up, while it structures the Eddard-Cersei conflict in *A Game of Thrones*, looks nothing like the narrative of the rest of *A Song of Ice and Fire* as it progresses. Most especially, Jon Snow is no Richard III. The question of who is supposed to be Martin's Richard III runs throughout all five phases of his engagement with the Tudor myth.

That question is answered, provisionally, in the second phase: the initial plan. Martin's leaked original outline for *A Song of Ice and Fire* explains that Jaime Lannister will be the Richard III: "Jaime Lannister will follow Joffrey on the throne of the Seven Kingdoms, by the simple expedient of killing everyone ahead of him in the line of succession and blaming his brother Tyrion for the murders."[2] One of Jaime's victims was going to be Sansa and Joffrey's baby, making Sansa a Margaret whose child is murdered by Jaime's Richard III. In this formulation, the Starks are not the Yorks: the Lannisters are. Starks and Yorks swapped their referents. Making Sansa into Margaret makes the Starks into the Lancasters. Making Jaime into Richard turns Lannisters into Yorks. Was the name game misdirection all along? The Targaryens were still the Tudors, but Martin's letter also revealed that Jon Snow has a hidden heritage. As later learned in the show, Jon is not the furthest in the line of succession for the Starks. He is, instead, the eldest of the Targaryens. His father isn't Eddard Stark; it's Rhaegar Targaryen (it is tempting to think Martin was aware of the Bastard whose royal parentage is revealed in Shakespeare's *King John*). Jon's mother is Lyanna Stark, Eddard's sister who was betrothed to Robert Baratheon but then secretly wed Daenerys's oldest brother, Rhaegar, meaning Jon Snow is really Aegon Targaryen, the rightful heir to the throne in the Targaryen line of succession (7.7). Now Jon—rather than Daenerys—becomes the *Song of Ice and Fire* stand-in for Henry VII, whose grandfather, Owen Tudor, himself had a secret marriage to Queen Catherine of Valois, widow of Henry V.

In this context, it makes sense that Martin would turn the Starks into the Lancasters because Jon (as Henry VII) descends from both Starks (figures for the Lancasters) and Targaryens (figures for the Tudors). We also know that, initially, Martin planned a romantic relationship between Jon (eldest of the T-s) and Arya (youngest of the -rks). "She realizes, with terror, that she has fallen in love with Jon," Martin wrote in his leaked letter. "Their passion will continue to torment Jon and Arya throughout the trilogy, until the secret of Jon's true parentage is finally revealed in the last book."[3] Following the original analogy, *A Song of Ice and Fire* likely would have been the story of Jaime (as Richard III) killing the child of Sansa (as Margaret), then scheming and murdering his way through his own family to become king—until he was unseated by Jon (as Henry VII), who creates peace through marriage to Arya (as Elizabeth of York). Among the problems here is that Daenerys is erased from the main narrative, becoming a footnote in the Targaryen story. From Martin's outline, it seems likely that the original plan was for Daenerys to defeat Jaime to take the iron throne at the end of the second book in the trilogy. Would Daenerys then take from Jaime the mantle of Richard III to Jon's Henry VII?

Some possible answers—read as: *alterations*—arose in the third phase we can consider: the changes Martin made as he wrote the narrative. He abandoned the romantic relationship between Jon and Arya early on, turning it into a close friendship. Jaime did not become king—did not become a Richard III. Cersei became Queen. Sansa did not have Joffrey's baby—did not become a Margaret. She became an Anne Neville to Ramsey Bolton's Richard III. Daenerys was still Henry VII: the secret of Jon's birth had not yet been revealed. The Targaryens remained the Tudors. Jaime did not turn against his own family. Tyrion did, strengthening his connection—as an irreverent clown born with a physical deformity—to Richard III. With Richard III now disseminated throughout the Lannisters—refracted in Jaime, Cersei, and Tyrion—they further became the Yorks as the Starks further became the Lancasters, receding from power and prominence in the narrative. In line with that development, Tyrion also became an Elizabeth of York by leaving the Lannisters (figured as the Yorks) for Daenerys (as Henry VII). Just as the Jon-Arya relationship had shifted from romantic to friendly, so too the connection between Daenerys and Tyrion was professional, not sexual. Soon, Jon and Daenerys fell in love. Perhaps, harkening back to his origin as a Stark far down in the line of succession, Jon would become the Elizabeth of York to Daenerys's Henry VII. As the show approached its final seasons, all signs were pointing to Daenerys (as Henry VII) defeating Cersei (as Richard III), after which the partnership with Tyrion (as one Elizabeth of York) and Jon (as another) would unite the rival families, ending civil war.

That possibility was upended in the fourth phase of Martin's engagement with the Tudor myth: the revelation of Jon Snow's parentage. Jon became the Henry VII figure, as always planned, yet the original plot structure surrounding him had changed, and this new revelation had to accommodate it. Jaime wasn't the Richard III of the original plan. Sansa wasn't the Margaret. Arya wasn't the Elizabeth of York. There were two major questions: (1) Who's the new Richard III? (2) Who's Daenerys meant to be? (Guess what: they're connected!).

As he wrote *A Song of Ice and Fire*, Martin disseminated the two key characteristics of Shakespeare's Richard III—(1) he's an irreverent noble mistreated because of his physical deformity, and (2) he's ambitious enough for sovereignty to murder his own family—to Tyrion and Daenerys. That's why Tyrion ended up on Team Dany. Tyrion took the psychological parts of Richard's story, Daenerys the political parts. We love Richard at the start of Shakespeare's play, though he does horrible things; later, when Richard becomes a tyrant, we have to negotiate our earlier affinity for the character. That is basically Daenerys in the fifth and final phase of Martin's engagement with the Tudor myth: the actual ending. We love her early in the story, not because (a la Richard and Tyrion) she's an irreverent clown, but because she's a freedom fighter and feminist icon. Then we have to wrestle with our affinity when she turns tyrant. Very Richard III. Cersei was never much of a Richard III. She became Queen, not by killing everyone between her and power, but by surviving all the death in her family. That makes Cersei back into the Margaret she was in the original set-up when she first killed Eddard Stark—making Lannisters back into Lancasters.

So Martin was golden: Dany and Tyrion as a composite Richard III would cut through Cersei and the Lan-family; Jon as Henry VII would come out of the dark with his hidden T-family claim to the throne and defeat them; and Arya as Elizabeth of York would partner with her close friend Jon to create peace, as planned from the beginning. That's why Daenerys, a Richard III figure, ultimately turned homicidal, and why Jon, a Henry VII figure, ended up killing, not marrying, her.

So what happened? How did Bran end up King of Westeros? Four factors seem most relevant. First, it's possible Martin's commitment to narrative unpredictability was more important than the historical parallel he had painstakingly mapped out, even if that parallel had narrative coherence. Second, it's plausible Martin's "tender spot in his heart for cripples, bastards, and broken things" led him to see the Bran-Tyrion administration as the ultimate disability "overcoming narrative" (sending disability scholars everywhere to their keyboards). Third, it's likely Martin wanted to reject the valorization of hereditary monarchy that would come with a Targaryen myth. Sam gets laughed at for proposing democracy, but the elective monarchy of the council is a move in that direction. Fourth, Martin probably couldn't resist, given his deep investment in history, crowning as king someone who symbolizes history (rather than, say, someone symbolizing bravery on the battle field [Jon], liberal politics [Dany], or even intelligence and virtue [Sansa]). So we get Bran as a Henry VIII of sorts, having the history of his empowerment written for him, favorably, with no heir in sight—with Jon, a Henry VII, and Tyrion, an Elizabeth of York, as his symbolic parents. The paradox is that, to crown history king, Martin had to depose the historical analogy to the Tudor myth that governed his story up to that point.

Notes

1 In 2005, Martin wrote that "anyone who thinks that by identifying my source material they can predict my plot is going to be severely misled" (quoted from Kavita Mudan Finn, "Game of Thrones is Based in History—Outdated History," *The Public Medievalist* [May 16, 2019], https://www.publicmedievalist.com/thrones-outdated-history/). I learned that the hard way after writing an essay titled "How Game of Thrones Will End: Spoilers from the Fifteenth Century," *Public Seminar* (April 24, 2019), http://publicseminar.org/2019/04/how-game-of-thrones-will-end/. It predicted Jon, as a Henry VII figure, would marry Daenerys, as an Elizabeth of York. Instead, she turned tyrant, and he killed her. It is entirely possible the shift away from the Shakespearean source is connected to the harsh response to the terrible writing in the final season of the show. I say this not as a bardolatrous aesthetic judgment but in coordination with Zeynep Tufekci's argument that the writing in *Game of Thrones* shifted from the more sociological storylines of the early seasons (where George R.R. Martin was the principle storyteller) to the more psychological stories of the later seasons (which were written by a hodgepodge of folks at HBO); see "The Real Reason Fans Hate the Last Season of Game of Thrones," *Scientific American* (May 17, 2019), https://blogs.scientificamerican.com/observations/the-real-reason-fans-hate-the-last-season-of-game-of-thrones/. Shakespeare could certainly do psychological turmoil, but ultimately he cared more about culture than character, especially in his history plays.
2 Kirsten Acuna, "Here's the Original 3-Page Outline George R.R. Martin wrote for 'Game of Thrones' in 1993," *Insider* (Aug. 14, 2017), https://www.insider.com/game-of-thrones-original-story-2017-8.
3 Acuna, "Here's the Original 3-Page Outline."

19 Fandom as IKEA effect

I often remind students that Shakespeare is supposed to be hard. If it weren't difficult, it wouldn't be valuable. When it's easy, it's not fun. But trained Shakespeare scholars and ardent Martin superfans alike can easily forget how extremely difficult and frustrating the first tetralogy and *Game of Thrones* can be to new audiences.

Four shared features stand out. First, these texts have a massive length and scope. According to data from the website *Open Source Shakespeare*, the average number of words in a Shakespeare play is 22,595.[1] If the first and second tetralogies are taken together, they are 199,428 words long. That means Shakespeare's representation of the Tudor myth, if viewed as a unified story, is nearly nine times as long as the typical Shakespearean story. Likewise, there are an average of 33 characters in one of Shakespeare's plays, whereas the plays presenting the Tudor myth involve a total of 404 characters.[2] That means Shakespeare's account of the Tudor myth presents more than 12 times the number of characters to keep track of than the average Shakespearean play. Comparably, according to some estimates, there is a median of about 64,000 words in all books, and an average of 89 characters in contemporary novels.[3] Yet the full series of *A Song of Ice and Fire* has been estimated to have 1,749,000 words and 2,302 characters.[4] While these numbers should be treated with caution, as they are not scientifically collected or fully comparable, they suggest *A Song of Ice and Fire* is more than 27 times longer than the typical novel, with more than 25 times as many characters to keep track of.

Second, the complex genealogies of these massive casts of characters require extensive family trees to comprehend. As Figure 1.1 shows, Shakespeare's first tetralogy is about one great-great-grandson of Edward III being dethroned by someone who is, on his father's side, the great-great-grandson of Edward III and, on his mother's side, Edward III's great-great-great-grandson; that man's son is then dethroned by someone who is, on his mother's side, the illegitimate great-great-great grandson of Edward III and, on his father's side, the grandson of the widow of Edward III's great-grandson. Comparably, as Figure 1.2 shows, *Game of Thrones* is about the grandson of Aegon V losing his crown to Aegon's great-grandson, who then passes the throne to someone he believes to be his own son (which would make him Aegon's great-great-grandson), but who in reality is the illegitimate child of his wife and her incestuous brother (meaning the boy has no blood relation to Aegon); that new king executes the uncle of the great-great-grandson of Aegon, leading the new king to be attacked by his purported father's brothers, who are themselves great-grandsons of Aegon, as well as the cousin and adopted brother of Aegon's great-great-grandson; when the young king dies, the throne passes to his even younger brother, who also appears to be a great-great-grandson of Aegon but is actually illegitimate; the throne then goes to their mother, the widow of one of Aegon's great-grandsons, but she comes into conflict with an alliance between two of Aegon's long lost descendants, a great-granddaughter and her nephew, a great-great-grandson of Aegon.

Third, both Shakespeare's first tetralogy and *Game of Thrones* build plots with plots within plots, like Russian nesting dolls. As Figure 19.1 shows, Shakespeare's first tetralogy involves three levels of nested plots. There is the top level of the international war between the English and the French, as played out in conflicts between Talbot and Joan, Richard Plantagenet and Joan, Henry VI and Charles VII, and then later Edward IV and Louis XI. Then there is the middle level of the civil war between the Lancasters and the Yorks, resulting in conflicts of Henry VI, Queen Margaret, and the Duke of Somerset on one side versus Richard Plantagenet and his sons on the other side. This level of conflict is most memorably captured in the emblematic battle scene where a Lancastrian son kills his Yorkist father, then another father discovers he has killed his own son. This level also generates the climatic war between the Earl of Richmond and Richard III. But then there is the lowest level of intra-family conflict on both sides of the mid-level civil war. Within the House of Lancaster, we see hostility between Gloucester and Winchester, Suffolk and Henry VI, Margaret and Eleanor, and Margaret and Henry VI, among others. Later, within the House of York, we see conflicts between Edward IV and his brother Clarence, then between Richard III and pretty much everyone (including Edward IV, Clarence, Queen Elizabeth, Edward V, the young Duke of York, the Woodvilles, Hastings, and Buckingham).

Fandom as IKEA effect 117

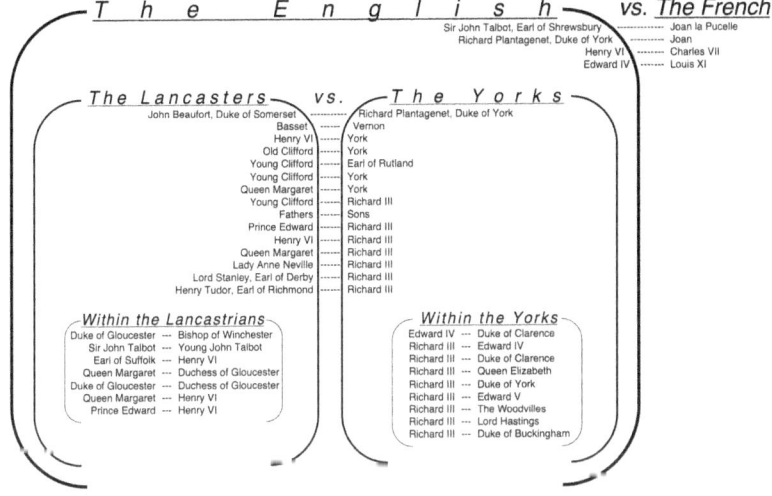

Figure 19.1 Shakespeare's first tetralogy: the nested plots.

Similarly, as Figure 19.2 shows, *Game of Thrones* involves four levels of conflict. There is the top level of the Great War between the living and the dead, as encapsulated in the conflict between Jon Snow and the Night King. Then there is a middle level of the intercontinental war between the Westerosi and the Targaryens, at first represented by Robert's aggression toward Daenerys, then later by Daenerys's aggression toward Cersei. There is also a lower middle level of the civil war among the Lannisters, the Starks, and the Baratheons, involving sub-plots pitting Ned against Cersei, Robb against Joffrey, Stannis against Joffrey, Breanne against Jaime, and Jon against Ramsey, among others. And finally there is the lowest level of the intra-family conflict within the warring houses: Robert versus Cersei, Stannis versus Renly, and Arya versus Sansa, for example. In both Shakespeare's histories and *Game of Thrones*, these nested plots generate much of the scope and intrigue of the texts, leading many characters—like Richard III and Jaime Lannister—to switch from protagonist to antagonist, or *vice versa*, as storylines expand and perspectives shift.

Fourth, amidst these nested plots, characters frequently shift allegiances, jumping from one side of a conflict to another. Naming only the major reconfigurations, in Shakespeare's first tetralogy, Burgundy defects from Talbot's English forces to Joan's French forces (*1 Henry*

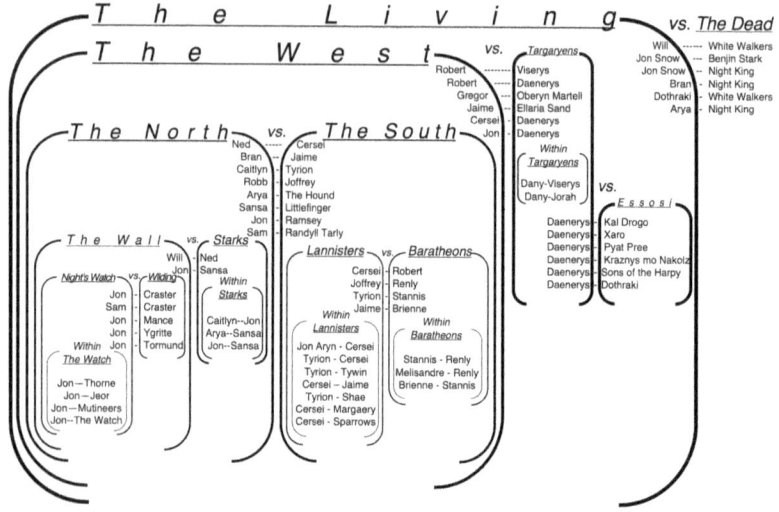

Figure 19.2 Game of Thrones: the nested plots.

VI, 3.7); the Parisians revolt against Joan and Charles (*1 Henry VI*, 5.3); Warrick defects from Edward IV to Louis XI (*3 Henry VI*, 3.3); Clarence defects from the Yorks to the Lancasters (*3 Henry VI*, 4.2), then defects back to the Yorks (*3 Henry VI*, 5.1); Lady Anne shifts from Lancastrian to Yorkist (*Richard III*, 1.2); and Stanley, Buckingham, and Queen Elizabeth each shifts from Yorkist to Lancastrian (*Richard III*, 4.2–4.5). A list of the shifting allegiances in *Game of Thrones* can only scratch the surface of what we see in the books: Rhaegar has his marriage to Elia Martell annulled so he can marry Lyanna Stark. Viserys sells off his sister Daenerys to Drogo. Daenerys and Drogo shift allegiance from Viserys to each other. Sansa bounces from a Stark to a Lannister to a Bolton and back. Littlefinger betrays Ned to Joffrey. Joffrey betrays his promise to Sansa to keep her father alive. Theon Greyjoy betrays the Starks and takes Winterfell. The Tyrells shift allegiances from the Baratheons to the Lannisters. The Tyrells then betray the Lannisters by poisoning Joffrey at his wedding. Walder Frey betrays the Starks at the Red Wedding, shifting allegiances to the Lannisters. Arya shifts from the Hound's prisoner to his protégé. Jaime betrays the Lannisters to set Tyrion free. Shea betrays Tyrion by becoming Tywin's lover. Tyrion then turns (along with Varys) from the Lannisters to Daenerys. Jon's sympathies seem constantly torn between the Night's Watch and the Wildings. After being empowered by Cersei, the faith militant turn on her. Stannis burns his own daughter at the stake. Theon is able to turn on his abuser, Ramsey Bolton, to save Sansa. The Night's Watch, including Olly, turn on Jon Snow and kill him. Littlefinger and the Knights of the Vale back Sansa rather than Ramsey. But then Littlefinger tries to pit Arya and Sansa against each other. The Sand Snakes kill Myrcella. Cersei aligns with Euron Greyjoy. Viserion is turned from Daenerys's dragon to a White Walker. And foes Daenerys and Cersei form an alliance to fight the White Walkers, though Cersei doesn't honor it.

My point with these lists is that both Shakespeare's first tetralogy and *Game of Thrones* are, simply put, difficult texts. They require lots of time and energy to understand. Genealogical charts, character maps, extensive notes, encyclopedias, and handbooks. Even for Shakespeare scholars professionally trained to interpret such things, or fans who go to *Game of Thrones* conventions, these texts are chaotic and confusing. Audiences driven by the quest for pure pleasure have every reason to dislike and ignore these texts.

Yet both texts have strong followings: those who like these texts *really* like these texts. With respect to the Wars of the Roses, the most notable fan culture is probably the Richard III Society, a group of enthusiastic amateur historians, founded in 1924, and now boasting international chapters, positioned against Shakespeare's slanderous portrait of their man.[5] More recently, there is the Twitter account @HollowCrownFans, which started as a fan space for the recent BBC adaptations of Shakespeare's history plays, but has grown into a fandom for all things Shakespeare, moderating the weekly #ShakespeareSunday where fans mash-up the English playwright with modern pop culture.[6] Studies by Kavita Mudan Finn, Anna Blackwell, Romano Mullin, Jessica McCall, Nora J. Williams, and Johnathan H. Pope show Shakespearean fandom to be surging, including (to quote Finn) a "small but prolific corner of the Internet devoted to Shakespeare's histories."[7] As for *Game of Thrones*, its fandom is legendary, including entire conventions where fans dress as their favorite characters and discuss, debate, and celebrate all things Westeros—representing, as Finn puts it, "the mainstreaming of fantasy fandom."[8] *Game of Thrones* has even been singled out as the number two fandom in the world by the website *Fan Sided*; it was number one but was recently bested by Ohio State Buckeyes fans, though *Game of Thrones* still beats out impressive fan cultures like Star Wars, Beyonce, Lebron James, and the Chicago Cubs.[9] The fandoms of Shakespeare and *Game of Thrones* even collide in the Twitter account @ShakesOfThrones, which puts

Game of Thrones dialog into Shakespearean language and posts *Game of Thrones* visuals for Shakespearean speeches, in addition to providing more traditional essays.[10]

Why do fans love these texts so intensely? Such investments may be problematic in light of scholarship seeing fan labor as exploitable and fan love as mockable.[11] But there is a connection between labor and love. The strong fan bases of both Shakespeare's history plays and *Game of Thrones* exhibit something called the IKEA effect.

Taking its name from the "assembly required" furniture store, the IKEA effect refers to a psychological phenomenon where people highly value things they have imbued with their own labor.[12] Researchers tested this notion in an experiment that divided people into two groups. One group was asked to build their own IKEA box. The other was given a pre-assembled box. When asked to estimate the value of the box, those who built their own boxes (even if those boxes showed shoddy workmanship) priced them 63 percent higher than those who didn't build the boxes themselves. So let's say I buy a bed for $500, and pay someone $50 to put it together. I might try to sell that bed a few years later for $250. But if, instead of paying someone, I had put the bed together myself, I might try to sell it—because of the IKEA effect—for $300. I like the bed and think it's more valuable because I remember putting my work into it. Exertion of effort on an object leads one to view that object as a sign of competency, leading to feelings of pride (and to opportunities for bragging rights). After confirming this phenomenon with a series of additional experiments, the researchers concluded that when people put their own labor into something, it increases their valuation of it, which has wide-ranging implications. It could mean, for example, that we don't work so hard to raise our children because we love them so much. Instead, we love our children so much because we've worked so hard to raise them.

And it could mean we love difficult texts like Shakespeare's first tetralogy and *Game of Thrones* precisely because they are so difficult. With their prodigious length, expansive scope, genealogical webs, nested plots, and shifting character allegiances, the extreme amount of work we have to put into understanding them leads us—because of the IKEA effect—to highly value what we have toiled over extensively. Our intellectual and emotional investment is registered by the enthusiasm with which we embrace these texts. We feel a sense of competence and pride in our hard-won ability to understand and explain the Wars of the Roses and the War of the Five Kings, and we want to share our expertise with others. If these texts weren't so hard, we wouldn't love them so much.

Notes

1 See "Shakespeare's Plays, Listed by Number of Words," *Open Source Shakespeare*, https://www.opensourceshakespeare.org/views/plays/plays_numwords.php.
2 See "Shakespeare Text Statistics," *Open Source Shakespeare*, https://www.opensourceshakespeare.org/stats/.
3 See Gabe Habash, "Average Book Length: Guess How Many Words Are in A Novel," *Huff Post* (March 9, 2012), https://www.huffingtonpost.com/2012/03/09/book-length_n_1334636.html; Andrew Piper, *Enumerations: Data and Literary Study* (Chicago: University of Chicago Press, 2018), 228n8.
4 The estimate of the number of words comes from "Wordcount of (un)popular (and hefty) Epics," *Looping World* (March 6, 2009), http://loopingworld.com/2009/03/06/wordcount/. The estimate of the number of characters comes from a spreadsheet created by the Reddit user Mynotoar; see Rand al'Thor, "How Many Named Characters Are There in A Song of Ice and Fire?" *Stack Exchange* (Jan. 19, 2016), https://scifi.stackexchange.com/questions/115429/how-many-named-characters-are-there-in-a-song-of-ice-and-fire.
5 See the Richard III Society, "About Us," http://www.richardiii.net/aboutus.php.
6 See Romano Mullin, "Tweeting Television/Broadcasting the Bard: @HollowCrownFans and Digital Shakespeares," in *Broadcast Your Shakespeare: Continuity and Change Across Media*, ed. Stephen O'Neill (London: Bloomsbury, 2018): 206–27.
7 Kavita Mudan Finn, "History Play: Critical and Creative Engagement with Shakespeare's Tetralogies in Transformative Fanworks," *Shakespeare* 13.3 (2017), 216; Anna Blackwell, *Shakespearean Celebrity in the Digital Age: Fan Cultures and Remediation* (New York: Palgrave Macmillan, 2018); Jessica McCall and Kavita Mudan Finn, "Exit, Pursued by a Fan: Shakespeare, Fandom, and the Lure of the Alternate Universe," in *Shakespeare and Creative Criticism*, ed. Rob Conkie and Scott Maisano (New York: Berghahn, 2019), 38–53; Nora J. Williams, "@Shakespeare and @TwasFletcher: Performances of Authority," *Humanities* 46 8.1 (2019); https://doi.org/10.3390/h8010046; and Johnathan H. Pope, *Shakespeare's Fans: Adapting the Bard in the Age of Media Fandom* (New York: Palgrave, 2020).
8 See the Introduction to *Fan Phenomena: Game of Thrones*, ed. Kavita Mudan Finn (Bristol: Intellect, 2017), 7.
9 See "Fandom 250," https://fansided.com/fandom250/page/50.
10 See @ShakespeareOfThrones on Twitter (https://twitter.com/shakesofthrones) as well as the blog at https://shakespeareofthrones.com.
11 See Abigail De Kosnik, "Fandom as Free Labor," in *Digital Labor: The Internet as Playground and Factory*, ed. Trebbor Schultz (New York: Routledge, 2013), 98–111; Casey J. McCormick, "Active Fandom: Labor and Love in the Whedonverse," in *A Companion to Media Fandom and Fan Studies*, ed. Paul Booth (Chichester: Wiley-Blackwell, 2018), 369–84; and Mel Stanfill, "Fandom and/as Labor," in *Exploiting Fandom: How the Media Industry Seeks to Manipulate Fans* (Iowa City: University of Iowa Press, 2019), 130–57.
12 See Michael I. Norton, Daniel Mochon, and Dan Ariely, "The IKEA Effect: When Labor Leads to Love," *Journal of Consumer Psychology* 22.3 (2012): 453–60.

Index

1 Henry IV 3, 27, 38, 50, 64
1 Henry VI 12, 37–38, 42, 50, 54, 70, 71, 74, 76, 86, 87, 93, 94, 118
10 Things I Hate about You 31
2 Henry IV 3, 38, 50, 64
2 Henry VI 37–38, 42, 45, 50, 54, 70, 71, 76, 81, 87, 93, 94
3 Henry VI 13, 37–38, 42, 54, 61, 67, 70, 71, 74, 79, 87–88, 93, 94, 118

acting 57–66, 103
adaptation 26–33
Addy, Mark 57
Alam, Roger 57
Anozie, Nono 57
Antony and Cleopatra 24, 64
Aristotle 53
Arryn, Jon 15
Austen, Jane 46
authorship: of *Game of Thrones* 38–39; of Shakespeare's history plays 37–38
Authur, Kate 49

Baelish, Petyr 3, 58, 118, 119
Bale, John 54
Baratheon, Joffrey 11, 15, 72, 95, 102, 106, 111, 112, 117, 118
Baratheon, Renly 15, 55, 77, 117
Baratheon, Robert 3, 15, 46, 58, 71, 72, 76, 95, 102, 104, 106, 111
Baratheon, Selyse 58
Baratheon, Shireen 86
Baratheon, Stannis 3, 15, 58, 77, 107, 117, 119
Baratheon, Tommen 72

Barton, John 26
BBC Television Shakespeare 26
Bean, Sean 57, 69
Beaufort, John, Duke of Somerset 42, 74
Beauty and the Beast, The 2
Becket, Thomas a 9–10
Bender, Jack 105
Benioff, David 4, 38, 48, 60, 92, 104
Beowulf 41
Biden, Joe 108
Blackwell, Anna 119
Bloody Hand, The 3
Bobono 102
Bolton, Ramsey 112, 117, 119
Bona, Lady of France 12–13, 67, 93
Bonneville, Hugh 32
Bradley, David 57, 63
Branagh, Kenneth 105
Breaking Bad 23, 32
Bridgman, Andrew 5
Brienne of Tarth 3, 58, 89
Broadbent, Jim 57
Brooke, Tom 57
Browning, Robert 27
Bruny, Gebrielle 49

Cade, Jack 42, 45, 50
Caldwell, Ellen C. 94
Cameron, James 54
Carroll, Shiloh 6, 19, 108
Césaire, Aimé 27
CGI 54–55, 57
Chaplin, Oona 58
Chaucer, Geoffrey 20
Christie, Gwendoline 3, 58

Christiensen, Jerome 38
Cibber, Colley 26
Clarence, Duke of 13, 15, 57, 116, 118
Clarke, Emilia 48, 57–58
Clifford, Old 42
Clifford, Young 42
Clinton, Hillary 74, 108
Cohn, Ruby 27
comedy 45, 48–50, 97
Comey, James 10, 72
Cooper, Helen 20
Costain, Thomas 17–19
Crane, Lady 58, 103, 105
Craster 59, 95
Cunningham, Liam 58
Cymbeline 20

Dance, Charles 58
Davenant, William 24, 26
David, Sara 48
Davis, Essie 58
Dawkins, Richard 30
Daxos, Xaro Xhoan 57, 96
Denslow, Kristin 30
Desmet, Christy 28
Dews, Peter 26
Dillane, Stephen 58
Dinklage, Peter 58, 81
Disney 19, 50
Doescher, Ian 27
Dondarrion, Beric 58
Dormer, Natalie 58
Dormer, Richard 58
Dothroki 77, 82, 83, 95, 96, 108
dragons 1, 4, 13, 41, 43, 55, 57–58, 82, 88, 90, 108
Drogo, Kal 95, 118
Dryden, John 24

early-modernism 20
Ebrose, Archmaester 57
Edmund of Langley, Duke of York 12
Edward I 10
Edward II 10
Edward III 10–11, 115–16
Edward IV 12–14, 15, 16, 31, 58, 67, 68, 93, 102, 116, 118
Edward of Lancaster, Prince of Wales 12–13, 15, 42

Edward the Black Prince 11
Edward the Confessor 9
Edward V 13, 15, 93, 116
Eleanor of Aquitaine 9
Eleanor, Duchess of Gloucester 42, 86–89, 93, 116
Eliot, T.S. 10
Elizabeth I 1, 14, 85, 89
Elizabeth of York 14, 93, 94, 111–13
Empire 23, 30, 31
Exeter, Duke of 59, 71, 76

Fabian, Robert 54
Fairley, Michelle 58
Famous Victories of Henry V 54
fan fiction 38, 90
fans 1, 3, 4, 49, 107, 115–20
Fantastic Four 2
fantasy 17, 19, 41–43, 46, 53–54, 57, 89, 90, 92, 96–97, 119
Fassbender, Michael 32
Fazel, Valerie 6, 30
Ferrell, Will 24
Fifty Shades of Grey 50
film 24, 26, 28, 50, 54, 60–61
Foinn, Kavita Mudan 6, 19, 87, 119
Fischlin, Daniel 30
Fitzgerald, Tara 58
Fletcher, John 27
focalization 45
Forbidden Planet 2, 24
Forel, Phario 102–03
Forel, Syrio 59
Frey, Lothar 57
Frey, Walder 57, 68
Fugelso, Karl 19

Garber, Marjorie 28
Garson, Barbara 27
Geddes, Louise 6, 30
generic bias 92–97
genre 17, 19, 41–46, 67, 80, 96–97, 105
"George R.R. Martin's Open Letter About the Deaths in *Game of Thrones*" 5
Gerzic, Marina 20, 32
Gillen, Aidan 58
Girls 51
Gjelsvik, Anne 89

Glen, Ian 58
Glover, Julian 58–66
Glover, Robert 59
Good Tickle Brain 4
Gosling, Mya 4
Grafton, Richard 53
Grant, Richard E. 59
Grenn 59
Gresham, Karen 88
Grey Worm 96
Greyjoy, Asha/Yara 3, 88
Greyjoy, Balon 59
Greyjoy, Euron 119
Greyjoy, Theon 118

Hadrian's Wall 41
Hall, Edward 53
Hall, Peter 26
Hamilton 26
Hamlet 3, 23, 24, 27, 30–31, 38, 50, 58, 59, 62, 63, 64, 65, 66, 101–05
Hansen, Adam 6, 29
Hardy, Mat 6
Harry Potter 54, 65
Hayles, N. Katherine 67
HBO 38–39, 48–49, 54, 55, 90, 103
Hendrick, Donald 30
Henry II 9
Henry III 10
Henry IV 3, 11–13, 15, 15, 58, 64
Henry V 11–12, 13, 58, 59, 70, 93
Henry V 2, 31, 38
Henry VI 12–13, 15, 42, 45, 58, 71, 72, 88, 93, 116
Henry VII 14, 15, 16, 42, 59, 68, 76, 93, 107, 110–13, 116
Henry VIII 1, 14, 16, 58
High Sparrow 59
Hill, Conleth 59–63
Hillman, Richard 94
Hinckley, David 32
Hinds, Ciarán 59
historical fiction 17, 19, 21, 43, 96
history plays 20, 26, 53–54, 67, 95, 96
Ho, Aaron K.H. 49
Hogarth Shakespeare series 24
Holderness, Graham 28–29
Holinshed, Raphael 53
Hollow Crown, The 26, 32, 69–70
@HollowCrownFans 119

Hotah, Areo 59
House of Cards 23, 30, 31
Howard, Jean 93
Humphrey, Duke of Glouchester 12, 15, 16, 42, 70–71, 76, 87, 116

IKEA effect 120
Iyengar, Sujata 28
Izembaro 59, 102–04

Jamison, Carol 20
Joan of Arc 12, 16, 42, 54, 70, 85–89, 93–94, 116, 117, 118
John of Gaunt, Duke of Lancaster 11, 12, 13, 58
John, King of England 10
Johnson, Samuel 46
Jones, Mark Lewis 59
Jones, Mike Rodman 20
Jonson, Ben 104
Jordan, Marjory 93
Julius Caesar 2, 3, 59, 65

Keats, John 27
Kendrick, Ellie 59
Kidnie, Margaret 28
King John 3, 111
King Lear 3, 23, 27, 31, 38, 50, 57, 58, 59, 65
Kirwin, Peter 29
Kurzel, Justin 32

Lamb, Charles and Mary 26
Lanier, Douglas 24, 29, 32
Lannister, Cersei 12, 15, 43, 61, 72, 77, 78, 81, 88–89, 95, 105–06, 110–13, 117, 119
Lannister, Jaime 3, 16, 111–12, 117, 118
Lannister, Tyrion 15, 43, 58, 72, 77, 79–82, 95, 96, 102–04, 106, 111–13, 118
Lannister, Tywin 16, 58, 81–82, 118
Lee, Stan 2
Legge, Thomas 54
Lesser, Anton 59–62
Levine, Nina S. 94
liberalism 74, 107–09, 113
Liedl, Janice 90
Lion King, The 24

Lloyd, Harry 59
Lord of the Rings, The 17, 54, 65
Lost 23, 32
Love's Labor's Lost 101
Lucy, William 75
Luhrmann, Baz 24
Luwin, Maester 59

Macbeth 3, 5, 26, 27, 31, 32, 38, 50, 57, 58, 59, 66
Malahide, Patrick 59
Margaret of Anjou, Queen 12, 15, 16, 61, 70, 76, 86–89, 93, 94, 110–13, 116
Marlowe, Christopher 37, 45, 50, 54, 93, 95
Marsden, Jean 27
Martell, Arianne 96
Martell, Elia 118
Martell, Oberon 59
Martin, George R.R.: biographical information 2, 17, 108; on the Wars of the Roses 1; use of history 1–2, 10, 110; use of Shakespeare 2–3, 21
Marvel 54
Matilda, Empress 9
Mawle, Joseph 59
MazDuur, Mirri 88
McCall, Jessica 119
McElhinney, Ian 59
McInnery, Tim 59
McNutt, Myles 48
medievalism 6, 19–20, 92
Melisandre 55, 89, 107
Menzies, Tobias 59
metatheater 101–06
Midsummer Night's Dream, A 101, 104
Missandei 96, 108
Mopatis, Illyrio 57
More, Thomas 53
Mormont, Jeor 77
Mormont, Jorah 58
Mormont, Lyanna 77
Morreall, John 50
Mortimer, Edmund 59
Msamati, Lucian 59
Much Ado About Nothing 4, 26, 50
Mullin, Romano 119

narrative relief 49–51
Needham, Jessica 49
neomedievalism 19–20
neoShakespeareanism 20
Neville, Anne 13, 16, 93, 112, 118
New Oxford Shakespeare 37
Night King 55, 78, 117
Night's Watch 77–78, 80, 109, 119
Norrie, Aidan 20
Not Shakespeare 21, 28–29, 30, 101–02, 104
nudity 48–51, 90, 104

Obama, Barack 108
Ophelia 24
Osha 59
Othello 3, 31, 38, 57, 59, 65

Pascal, Pedro 59
Pericles 20, 59
Petrarch 19
Plantagenet dynasty 9–14
Plantagenet, Geoffrey 9
Polanski, Roman 3
Pope, Johnathan H. 119
popularity 20, 53–55, 67–68
Porter, Cole 27
prince who was promised 13, 108
Pryce, Jonathan 59
Pugh, Robert 59
Pycelle, Grand Maester 58

Qyburn 59, 62

Rabkin, Norman 96
Rackin, Phyllis 93
Raff 103
rape 49, 81, 82, 89, 90, 95, 104
Rayder, Mance 59
Reduced Shakespeare Company 26
Reed, Meera 59
Reilly, John C. 24
Reynolds, Bryan 30
rhetorical misogyny 89–90
Richard I 10
Richard II 11–13, 15, 19, 57, 64, 65
Richard II 38
Richard III 2, 13, 16, 19, 20, 31, 42, 58, 59, 79–82, 88, 93, 102–03, 107, 110–13, 116, 117

Richard III 2, 3, 13–14, 15, 23, 26, 31, 37, 42, 64, 76, 87, 93, 102–03, 118
Richard III Society 119
Richard, Duke of York 12–13, 15, 16, 42, 67, 69–71, 74–76, 110, 116
Richmond, Earl of see Henry VII
Rigg, Diana 59
Rodgers, Amy 3
Roman, Christopher 108
romance 42–43, 46
Rome 51
Romeo and Juliet 2, 23, 24, 26, 27, 31, 57, 58, 59, 65
Rossini, Manuela S. 93
Rous, John 53
Royal Shakespeare Company 26
Russell, Clive 59

Saan, Salladhor 59, 95
Sand, Ellaria 59
Sawyer, Robert 28
Schwarz, Kathryn 93
Schwyzer, Philip 20
Seaworth, Davos 58, 77–78
Selmy, Barristan 59
sexposition 48–49
Shacklock, Zoë 38
Shadwell, Thomas 24
Shagga 59
Shakespeare for theory 6
Shakespeare in Love 27, 37
Shakespeare, William 30, 32; see also play titles
Shakespeare's first tetralogy 2; length 115; genealogies 11, 115–16; nested plots 116; shifting allegiances 117–18
Shakespeareanism 20
Shakespearean slingshot 23–24, 30–33
Shippey, Tom 19
Sir Gawain and the Green Knight 41
Snow, Jon 3, 16, 43, 68, 77–78, 79–81, 96, 107–09, 110–13, 117, 119
Somerset, Duke of 42, 74–75, 116
Song of Ice and Fire, A 1: parallels to the Wars of the Roses 1, 3–5, 14, 69, 79, 110–13; length 115;

genealogies 14, 116; nested plots 117; shifting allegiances 118–19
Sonnets 2
Sons of Anarchy 23, 30–31
Sparei, DeObia 59
spectacle 53–55
Spielberg, Steven 54
Stanley, Mark 59
Stanton, Kay 93
Star Trek 65
Star Wars 27, 50, 54, 63, 65, 119
Star-Crossed 23, 30, 31
Stark, Arya 16, 55, 88, 95, 101–06, 110–13, 117, 118, 119
Stark, Benjin 59
Stark, Bran 46, 95, 113
Stark, Catelyn 16, 46, 58, 89
Stark, Eddard 12, 16, 46, 57, 67–71, 95, 110, 111, 113
Stark, Robb 12, 16, 68, 117
Stark, Sansa 16, 89, 95, 104, 111–13, 117, 118, 119
Stark, Talisa 58, 68
stigmatized protagonist 79–83
Stoppard, Tom 27, 105
Stow, John 53
Suffolk, Earl of 12, 15, 42, 76, 87, 116
Sumpter, Donald 59

Talbot, Sir John 42, 54, 75, 93, 94, 116, 117
Talbot, Young 42
Talladega Nights: The Ballad of Ricky Bobby 24
Taming of the Shrew, The 27, 31, 101
Taneja, Preti 27
Targaryen myth 14, 107–09, 113
Targaryen, Aegon V 116
Targaryen, Aerys II 13, 15
Targaryen, Daenerys 12, 15, 43, 46, 55, 57–58, 77–80, 82–83, 86, 88, 95, 96, 107–08, 110–13, 117, 118, 119
Targaryen, Viserys 59, 77, 118
Teale, Owen 59
television 23–26, 38, 49, 51, 54, 61, 89
The Tempest 2, 24, 27, 101, 105
The Troublesome Reign of John, King of England 54

Tena, Natalia 59
Thorne, Allister 59
Tillyard, E.M.W. 11
Titus Andronicus 3
Tolkien, J.R.R. 3, 17, 43
tragedy 41–43, 64, 93, 97, 102
Trant, Meryn 55, 103
True Blood 51
True Detective 51
Trump, Donald 10, 72, 74
Tudor myth 11–14, 19, 20, 42–43, 92, 107–13; *see also* Wars of the Roses
Tudor, Henry *see* Henry VII
Tudor, Owen 13, 111
Tully, Brynden 59
Tully, Edmure 59
Tully, Samwell 63
Tyrell, Margery 58, 89, 95
Tyrell, Olenna 59, 106

Udall, Tom 108
Updike, John 27
Upstart Crow 32
Utz, Richard 19

Varma, Indira 59
Varys 3, 59, 118
Venning, Dan 4
Venus and Adonis 3
Verdi, Giuseppe 26
Vergil, Polydore 53
Vice Principals 30, 31–32
violence 49, 53, 104–05

Walker, Jessica 3
Walton, Priscilla L. 109
wars of roses 74–78; parallels to *A Song of Ice and Fire* 1, 3–5, 14, 69, 79, 110–13; as phrase 17; *see also* Tudor myth
Warwick, Earl of 13, 16, 42, 58, 75
Weiss, D.B. 4, 38, 48, 60, 92, 104
Wells-Lassagne, Shannon 51
Wells, Stanley 38
West Side Story 24
Westworld 32, 51
Wetmore, Kevin 6, 29
Wheel of Fortune 3, 41–43, 72
White Walkers 43, 46, 55, 57, 77, 80, 119
Will 32
William Shakespeare's Romeo + Juliet 23
William the Conqueror 9
Williams, Deanne 20
Williams, Nora J. 119
Winchester, Bishop of 42, 70, 76, 116
Woodville, Elizabeth 13, 67, 68, 93, 116, 118

X-Men 66
Xho, Jalabhar 96

Yerolemou, Miltos 59
Young, Helen 6
Young, Joseph 43

For Product Safety Concerns and Information please contact our EU representative GPSR@taylorandfrancis.com
Taylor & Francis Verlag GmbH, Kaufingerstraße 24, 80331 München, Germany

www.ingramcontent.com/pod-product-compliance
Lightning Source LLC
Chambersburg PA
CBHW051752230426
43670CB00012B/2248